Library Automation
For
21st Century

Library Automation For 21st Century

R.S. Aswal

Ess Ess Publications

4837/24, Ansari Road
Darya Ganj
New Delhi-110 002
Phone: 23260807, 41563444
Fax: 41563334
E-mail: info@essessreference.com
url: http://www.essessreference.com

First Published **2006**

ISBN: 81-7000-492-6

Rs Ess Ess Rs.650/-

Published by:
Ess Ess Publications
4831/24, Ansari Road, Darya Ganj, New Delhi-110 002
Tel: 011-23260807, 41563444 Fax: 011-41563334
E-mail: info@essessreference.com
url: www.essessreference.com

Printed in India at:
Printline, New Delhi

Contents

Preface

This book is divided into five parts; each part has been appropriately structured in Chapter 01 to Chapter 14.

Part I: Library Automation consists of three chapters. Chapter 1. Covers the History, need and purpose of Library Automation. Chapter 2 Planning, Implementation and Evaluation and Chapter 3 for Library Software and Hardware.

Part II: Retrospective Conversion. Chapter 4 and 5 describe the means of retrospective conversion for 21st century and the retrospective conversion process with new technology.

Part III. Integrated Library Systems. Chapter 6 to 9 describing the housekeeping operation in libraries. These include acquisition, Cataloguing, Circulation and Serial controls.

Part IV. Automated Information Services. Chapter 10 to 11, consist the OPAC/Web OPAC and automated services.

Part V. Technology Trends in Library. Chapter 12 to 14, describe the latest technology trend of digitization, advance bar coding system and Radio Frequency Identification technology.

This book is a guide for library professionals about the planning, Implementation and Evaluation process for a library automation system of all sizes for 21st century.

Acknowledgements

My primary gratitude and sincere thanks to Dr. Shankar Singh, Sr. Manager (Lib & Inf. Services) Central Public Sector, PFC; New Delhi for his transcendent suggestions, consistent support and continuous motivation. I am thankful to my colleagues of VTLS Pvt. Ltd., who supported and encouraged me. I would like to personally thank to my wife who motivated and cooperated me. My special thanks to my publishers M/S Ess Ess Publication for their cooperation and untiring efforts in bringing out this book in excellent form in short time.

I request the readers to convey the feedback along with any suggestion, comments and criticism for further improvement of this book.

Introduction

Library automation is the use of computers to control processes and replacing human operators. It is the technology concerned with the design and development of process and system that minimize the necessity of human intervention in their operation. It refers to the computerization or mechanization of all library activities, such as acquisitions, circulation, cataloging, serials, and an OPAC (online Public Access Catalog). Some advantages are repeatability, tighter quality control, waste reduction, and integration with business systems, increased productivity and reduction of labors. Some disadvantages are high initial costs and increased dependence on maintenance.

Library automation in the 21st Century is on interconnecting systems, sharing information resources through innovative networking and ensuring equitable access to a broad range of information and users. These developments include the growth of the use of networks and the Internet. Library automation has changed the definition of the Librarians and the Library.

Librarians in the 21st Century will work in a broad spectrum of libraries and information centers, in the information industry, and in other venues where skills working with information content are needed. They must be able to understand and interpret an increasingly complex information environment; they must be able to collaborate effectively with other information professionals; they must be able to articulate the value of the knowledge and skills of librarianship in a rapidly changing information environment; and they must be competent managers capable of innovation, efficiency, and leadership as they meet the demands of their clientele.

The challenges of librarianship in the 21st Century including:

* Planning and implementing of the high quality library and information services in the changing social and technological environment of the 21st Century.
* Organizing libraries, media centers, and information agencies

to serve their clientele effectively.

* Designing information systems that meet specific needs of library and information users.
* Integrating information technologies creatively and effectively into library and information services.
* Developing techniques to organize and retrieve vast amounts of information.
* Increasing the effectiveness of libraries as a foundation in preserving a nation's cultural heritage.
* Sharing information resources through innovative networking and ensuring equitable access to a broad range of information.

It is necessary for librarians to keep a watch on the developments and to choose appropriate technology depending on the needs. Also, it is very important for librarians to interact with computer professionals as the library automation at all levels needs good co-ordination between both these professionals.

Libraries: Library without wall is the vision of 21st century. The definition of library has totally been changed, and not limited to storage of books. The forms of the library collection have also been changed and rapidly converting in the safe of digital format.

This book is a guide for library professionals about the planning process for a library automation system of all sizes. The library needs are more sophisticated, if your current library automation system is not fit for latest technology environment of 21st century and your library system doesn't work properly, you should look at new library systems. Seize this opportunity to assess your library's mission, look at your current capabilities and expertise, and analyze how a new library system can help you meet your service goals.

Part I : Library Automation

Chapter 1
History, Need and Purpose of Library Automation

1.1 History of Library Automation

In 1930s, the efforts of library automation system was started by Herman Hollerith of the US Census Bureau who invented punched card technology, with the help of Dr. Jolul Shaw Billings, the then Director of Surgeon-General's Library (now the National Library of Medicine). In 1935, Dr. Ralph H. Parker Created a circulation control system at the University of Texas at Austin using the Hollerith Punched Card or IBM Punched card equipments. However due to slow progress in the development of computer systems the efforts was put into experimental project of library automation system.

In 1960s the first trend of library automation was developed in US, using computers for creating bibliographic databases as library catalogues. Library of congress developed a machine-readable catalogue of its holdings records using the MARC input format. In 1967 the OCLC (Online Computer Library Center), was started the first computer-based library network.

During the 1970s the development of the integrated computer chip and storage devices led to an explosion of library automation. RLIN (Research Libraries Information Network) and WLN (Washington Library Network) was started the online library networks. In this decade, a number of libraries started automation using the microcomputers of their organizations.

During 1980s, when the rapid development of lower cost microcomputers and its easily available in libraries, the automation became a possible proposition for all types and sizes of libraries. Many library automation packages also came into the market. The introduction of CD-ROMs in the late 1980 has changed the way libraries operate, CD-ROMs containing databases, software, and information previously only available through print, became available making the information more accessible.

The 1990s have seen the rise of computer networking. By linking computers together to form a network, access can be provided both locally and from a distance, and the different resources held on the networked computers can be shared. Libraries also stared Internet and the World Wide Web on a large-scale providing quick library and information services to their users. Also, hardware-specific automation packages, packages with web-interface, came into the market.

In the new millennium, every library, small medium or large are now using the computers and plans or implements automation of its activities and services. Computerized catalogues or OPACs largely replace traditional library catalogues. Technological advances will continue to open new opportunities for libraries to provide efficient and exhaustive information services and to link to computer networks worldwide. The latest technology penetration in library automation system is barcode technology, digital library and RFID security system. The library automation, which started in the 1970s in a few special libraries, has now reached most of the special and universities libraries. It is yet to take off in college libraries in India owing to various problems.

1.2 Need and Purpose of Library Automation

The motto of library automation is to provide the write information, to write person, in write manner, in write time. While justifying need for library automation more than cost-effectiveness the benefits derived by the library users become the major consideration. Since library does not happen to be an economic entity such benefits need to be looked at in a different perspective. To appreciate the advantages it becomes necessary to highlight the different levels of library automation. For convenience it can be visualized at following levels:

1.2.1. Library cataloguing system

The automated library cataloguing system means creation of bibliographical information in MARC standard format for most of the library activities and services such as acquisition, reference, bibliographic service, inter-library loan, cooperating cataloguing, etc.. For user point of view, users can search any fields, fast retrieval and printing the required information. User can also use to access the same database, e-mail services, make their request/reserve and other internet services, if the same system is available in network environment.

MAchine Readable Cataloging records are the standard method of storing and transmitting bibliographic records. The Library of Congress, OCLC and RLG create most bibliographic records in MARC standard. Each utility offers MARC record distribution services. Records that come from Library of Congress, and OCLC are usually of high quality. Other sources may not supply records that are as complete. If your records are of lesser quality, then you may want to have them enhanced by cataloging utility's software before adding them to your database.

1.2.2. To reduce the staff

Library automation means minimize the intervenes of human activities and maximizes the uses of latest technology. It's eliminating the repetitive work and cumbersome job of printing the card catalogue. It save the stationary and space. It reduces the activities of human being in all the housekeeping operation and makes the process simple.

1.2.3. Increase the staff productivity

It increase the efficiency and productivity of library staff by using copy cataloguing, sharing of bibliographical records, making union catalogue, use of other external databases. It makes the consistency of the record and the standard quality.

1.2.4. Housekeeping operations

Housekeeping operations covers acquisition, circulation and serial control, cataloguing. The all these features should be required in the library software. The Circulation Data Migration facilities should be required it reflects your collection's use, and is a valuable resource for library managers. Charge and hold transactions offer a timely picture of what items are popular and in use, while other data (fines paid, items declared lost, etc.) gives the library long-term management tools to control library resources.

1.2.5. Advance in technology

Library should follow the new advance technology i.e. RFID. A new and innovative replacement for barcode technology is RFID (Radio Frequency Identification Devices). RFID is used in retail environments, and is beginning to be installed in libraries. RFID brings many of the same advantages of barcodes, but uses a different type of reader to collect data. When this technology is used in libraries it allows books to be checked out and returned without the need to physically handle every item. In addition, it makes library inventory projects much more efficient. Instead of pulling each book off the shelf to scan a barcode, an RFID reader is simply passed near the shelf and all the RFID labels are read and decoded.

1.2.6. System hardware and software

A computer operating system is the underlying software that is usually provided by the hardware manufacturer from whom you purchased your system. Arguments outlining advantages and disadvantages of operating systems are beyond the scope of this document. Most library system vendors offer software that runs on more than one operating system platform.

1.2.7. Access to external information through Internet

If your library does not yet have an installed TCP-IP based telecommunications network, you should immediately take steps to plan for one and have it installed. Network planning is beyond the scope of this document. However, every library system on the market today uses TCP-IP as its basic telecommunications structure, so without such a network, no library software can operate. If your library has a TCP-IP network, make sure that the cabling connecting workstations to routers in each branch is Level 5 or above (Cat 5, Cat5E, or Cat6). Any cabling under Cat5 is susceptible to electronic interference and to data corruption.

1.2.8. Meet specific needs of library and information users

Your library system contains personal information about your patrons and their transactions, as well as invaluable information about your library's holdings, and the status of each item. Without this information, the library would not be able to operate. All networks are potentially vulnerable to intrusion from hackers. At a minimum, your network should be protected by a firewall that shields your telecommunications equipment and servers from external attack by closing down access to all ports except those necessary for system operations.

1.3. Barriers of Library Automation

Following could be the few possible barriers of library automation:

1.3.1. Fear of adverse impact on employment

If we analyze the various jobs such as book acquisition, technical processing, circulation and reference service one can conclude that human interference is necessary at each and every step. The only area where substantial manpower can be saved is the cataloguing. The data entered at the time of ordering can be used for cataloging with some updating would eliminate multiple card preparation and subsequent filing. The manpower thus saved can be utilized in retrospective conversion and later on for analytical cataloguing or introducing new services. Therefore, there will be no adverse impact on employment.

1.3.2. Apprehension that the technology could be too expensive

There is an apprehension that the technology, both hardware and software would be expensive and unaffordable. The cost of hardware and software depends on the level of automation. From the user point of view cataloguing system is most important and also forms the base for other library activities. Keeping these two points in view INFLIBNET developed a PC based software titled 'SOUL' is available at a very nominal price in India. Besides this 'CDS/ISIS' and 'KOHA' MARC based open software are available.

1.3.3. The library staffs have to undergo extensive training

The in-house training for handling the software is usually provided by the vendor who supplied the software. However, training for CDS/ISIS is available at NISCAIR, INFLIBNET and DRTC. The training of library staff also depends on the level of automation. If one decides to go only for cataloguing a minimum training of one or two weeks duration will enable the librarians to develop a database and maintain it. With this basic training one can easily transfer the same data on a server/main machine in a network environment.

1.3.4. Lack of support from the management, may be owing to budget constraints

The lack of support from the management, may be owing to budget constraints, will be one of the barriers. Here the role of librarians becomes crucial in convincing the management that the users of libraries will also be the major beneficiaries of automation. Also, the skill and initiative play a major role in convincing the management.

1.3.5. Fifth reason could be retrospective conversion of data

The manpower saved could be utilized for retrospective conversion and later on for analytical cataloguing. However, most of the libraries have taken time bound project for this purpose.

1.4. Selection of Library Software

If a library wants to make a beginning; CDS/ISIS, KOHA or SOUL is best suited as it involves minimum investment on both hardware and software. Once a database with bibliographic details is developed, the same data can be used for circulation activities. Here the selection of software becomes crucial because CDS/ISIS and KOHA is a open source software and nobody can give the proper attention for maintenance. SOUL is good package but its need more feature such as ISO 2709 format, web interface and compatibility of digital and security system. So librarians should keep in mind the following criteria to select the right software for library housekeeping operations:

* Who are the developers, whether an institution, or reputed company or few individuals. The preference is for institution and second preference is for the reputed company.
* How many times the software has been revised since the time of its first launch.
* How many parameters are available for each module. More the parameters better will be the flexibility and needs no or minimum customization.
* Whether the software has facility to import bibliographic data available in ISO2709 format and similarly export of data in this format.
* Training and guidance after installation.
* Whether available on major operating systems.
* Whether it is web interface.
* Whether it can be interfaced with the e-mail system of the campus network.
* Whether it has taken care of Y2K compliant.
* How many installations it has got in the country, since when and major clients.

* Whether it can offer OPAC and different rights to different logins.

1.5. Automated Library System

An automated library system usually consists of a number of functional modules, such as acquisitions, circulation, cataloging, serials, and an OPAC (Online Public Access Catalog). An "integrated" library system is an automated system, as described above, in which all of the functional modules share a common bibliographic database. The National Library of Medicine used the term "integrated" in referring to a system in which all automated library functions are processed against a single, master bibliographic file.

In a system, which is not integrated, there might be a bibliographic record in the catalog for a book and, if that book were to be checked out, there would be another bibliographic record for it in a circulation file. In an integrated system, there would be one bibliographic record for a book, probably created when the book was ordered, then expanded when it was cataloged. If that book were to be checked out, the patron record for the borrower would be attached to the bibliographic record, but there would not be a duplicate bibliographic record for the book in a circulation file. There are some systems which have duplicate bibliographic records but which are considered to be integrated because changes to bibliographic records are automatically propagated. For example, a change made to a bibliographic record in the acquisitions file would automatically be made to the duplicate bibliographic record in the catalog. In these quasi-integrated systems, some type of linking mechanism facilitates movement between the modules and their duplicate files.

There are several different ways the integration of a system can be accomplished. A library can:

* Buy an integrated system, including a number of functional modules, from a single vendor;
* Purchase a variety of modules from a variety of vendors and interconnect them; or

* Implement any number of purchased modules, from either one or multiple vendors, and then connect them to sources of information outside the library.

1.5.1 What are the advantages of an integrated system?

An integrated system is superior in several ways to one, which is not integrated.

* The duplication of effort to create and maintain multiple copies of bibliographic records is eliminated in an integrated system.
* Opportunities for errors are reduced when records are entered only once, and changes are automatically propagated throughout the system.
* Library staff and patrons can have access to all pertinent information at one location.

For example, in an integrated system, a patron can view a bibliographic record in the online catalog and also see that the book has been checked out and when it is due back to the library. Of course, preventing patrons from viewing borrower information can protect privacy of borrowers. Also, patrons can tell by looking at the online catalog, in an integrated system, that a book has been ordered, but not yet received. In a system, which is not integrated, that information would be available to library staff only through the acquisitions module.

1.5.2 How does a library select an integrated system?

There are many vendors of integrated systems. One source for information on vendors and systems is "Automated System Marketplace" which is published annually in Library Journal. While it is possible, using such a tool, to identify market leaders among the vendors, it is not possible to say which of the available systems is best. Such a determination would have to be based on a thorough understanding of the library for which the system was intended and of that library's needs and resources. A system, which might be ideal for a large academic library, would not be suitable for a small school library. Still, the number of systems, which a vendor has installed, is one measure of success and quality. Other measures include level of customer support provided and customer satisfaction.

There are also a number of system performance issues, which must be addressed during the selection process. Does the system have the capacity to handle the number of transactions, e.g. the number of books checked out daily, in the library without slowing to an unacceptable level of performance? How many bibliographic records and patron records can the system hold?

Also, libraries must look to the future when purchasing a system. How much growth, in terms of patrons and materials, can the system accommodate? Will the library be able to migrate from this system to another system without extensive redesign of the database?

1.5.3 Implementation and management issues

Just as important as, or perhaps more important than, selecting the right system is the process of implementing that system in the library and dealing with the associated management issues. As described above, one of the main features and advantages of an integrated system is the sharing of bibliographic records among the various system modules. This single feature can have far reaching implications for the management of the library. Some organizational changes, which have accompanied the implementation of integrated systems, include:

* New patterns of communication among library staff, especially between technical services staff and public services staff;
* Increases in responsibility and decision making among lower level staff; and
* Increased requirements for all staff to acquire technical knowledge and skills.

Many libraries have redesigned their operations to take maximum advantage of the new technology.

1.5.4 Future trends in integrated library systems

The definition of an integrated system is beginning to change from a system, which shares bibliographic records among local functions and modules to a system, which exchanges information with many other systems outside of the library. Technological developments, such as client/server architectures and standardized protocols for passing information from one system to another, are facilitating this integration of outside information sources into local systems. For example, an online ordering system might allow a librarian to search a publisher's bibliographic database, select records of books to be purchased, and download those records from the publisher's database into the library catalog. Also, some libraries with expanded integrated systems offer patrons access, through their local OPACs, to other bibliographic and non-bibliographic databases both inside and outside the library and to OPACs of other libraries.

Chapter 2
Planning, Implementation and Evaluation

2.1. Planning

All library automation projects shall have a project implementation plan. Planning for an automated system, no matter how big or small, should be part of an overall long-range plan for the library. Automation should always be used as a means to achieve overall better patron service. Careful planning for technology will assure that your automation project is "sustainable", i.e. enhances the organization's ability to meet its service mission without disrupting the organizational stability of the institution.

As applicable, it is recommended that project implementation plans include, but not be limited to.

2.1.1 Describing existing library procedures

Before designing new automated systems, one should study the existing systems. This study may help us to know how current work is carried on and the problems involved there in. The following thing should keep in mind

* Which processes are repetitive and occupy large amounts of staff time?
* Which require retrieval of information from large difficult to maintain files?
* Which services place the biggest load on staff?
* Which are most popular with patrons?

For each functional area determine

* Current workflow patterns and procedures.
* How much space and equipment are used.

* Volume of activity.
* Cost to perform
* Current problems or needs in the area.
* Set priorities for what services to automate in a phased approach.
* Begin defining the steps for a phased and coordinated plan to automate.
* Analyze hardware, software, telecommunications needs.
* Identify start-up and ongoing costs for automation plan.
* Develop a budget for automation

2.1.2 Assessing needs and setting priorities

To assess the library's needs for automation. This data will be used for a variety of purposes throughout the planning process. Including, when you are preparing a preliminary cost estimate, providing information for an RFP, calculating the storage requirements for your new system. If you do not have some of this information there are ways to reasonably estimate the data. Important to remember that large amounts of time need not be devoted to determining a perfectly exact number. Careful estimates can suffice for planning purposes.

Tasks

* Study, analyze, and document the current system including review of policy and procedure manuals, training manuals, and workflow diagrams.
* Begin to communicate with staff and users about library automation (committee for involving staff in planning, staff survey, user survey or focus groups).
* Collect and compile narrative and statistical information necessary to describe Library system and its operations.
* Assess the library's service mandates.
* Assess the library's operating environment including facilities, budget, community relations, and interlibrary cooperative arrangements.

2.1.3 Feasibility studies

This feasibility studies determining whether or not the proposed library automation project will be technically, operationally and economically feasible. It's depend upon the size of the library.

* *Technical feasibility* : What is a existing library technology and what's will be changed? It will be suitable for library or not, or it can be customized as per library need. The hardware and software for proposed project should be technical guarantees of accuracy, reliability, security, etc. in the new technology.
* ***Operational feasibility*** : This study of operational feasibility is to examine whether the proposed project/ system will work when it is developed and installed or whether there is any barrier to implementation.
* ***Economic feasibility*** : The study of economic feasibility is to determine, whether the proposed project is economically viable or not.

2.1.4 Find a library that has automated

Now the BIG question! What System Should I Buy or what is the BEST for me? You should visit other libraries that are of similar size and staff that have already gone through the process of automating. Typically, these libraries have worked the bugs out and already made the mistakes. Making a site visit can learn a lot.

Find a library that has automated and make an appointment to go and work for free for them for a day so you can get the feel of how they use their catalog system. This is the way you may decide that you either do or do not like this particular automation system.

Obtain a list of automation vendors and send out a request for information to each vendor that seems appropriate. This request would be like a one page resume of your library and include basic statistics, such as your library service area, title count, circulation count, number of staff and so forth.

Also, you may try to ask for a ballpark figure (not legally binding) of the costs for implementing their product based on your request for information.

Initially, consider all the automation systems that respond to your request for and seem appropriate for your library. Then, narrow down your list to 2 or 3 products. Then, invite the remaining 2 or 3 vendors' sales representatives to your library for a demonstration of their product.

Always ask the vendor for a client list so you can call those libraries to find out if they are happy with their system.

2.1.5 Hiring a consultant, if big project

The purpose of hiring a consultant is to support a library's planning for automation that would include:

> Developing an infrastructure for communicating with all participants in the planning process, defining the problem you hope to address through automation, needs assessment, determination of staffing needs and financial resources, project budget preparation, assistance with technical aspects of planning that go beyond the library's staff experience or expertise, vendor & system performance evaluation, and contract and purchase negotiation.

The expenditure of money for a consultant will more than pay for itself in avoiding delays, facilitating staff effectiveness and getting the most from your planning process. The important thing to remember is that when you hire a consultant you are entering into a partnership with a knowledgeable professional with the skill and experience necessary for a successful project. You do not give up autonomy in decision-making, nor are you hiring an extra hand to do all the planning work for you. It is a partnership in which you and your staff will be expected to contribute a great deal.

Gathering the data necessary for describing your library's needs can be complex. A consultant can bring a proven data collection method to your needs assessment and evaluation process. Describing your needs accurately is important to assure that the system you purchase is not under-configured from the outset and will guarantee that your performance expectations are compatible with the system purchased and adequate for long-term growth.

2.1.6 Bibliographic database development

To establish a complete database of all libraries holdings that can be ready to load when the new library system is installed.

Tasks

* Identify, describe, and document existing shelf list files and begin to standardize the data they contain.
* Institute quality control measures to assure consistency of entries within the shelf list file.
* Inventory the collection.
* Verify existing bibliographic information in the shelf list records.
* Locate and add any necessary missing bibliographic information to the records.
* Implement uniform standardized cataloging practices and consistent uttering practices.
* Prepare specifications for treatment of bibliographic data and item data (including authority control needs).
* Prepare and distribute a Request for Proposals for vendor supplied data conversion project (including authority control)
* Evaluate proposals and select a vendor.
* Organize staff and define procedures for working with vendor to resolve bibliographic record conflicts.
* Weed your collection so you do not pay to catalog items that need discarding.
* How many titles do you circulate monthly?
* How many patrons do you have and how sophisticated

are they? Are most of your patron's university students and professors that do research or are they patrons that like to read for pleasure?

2.1.7 System specifications and requirements

To prepare an RFP with specifications for an automated system that will meet the service objectives and requirements for the County Library System.

Purpose of an RFP : to enable you to compare relative differences from one system to another. It is very difficult to do this only through vendor demonstrations, talking to sales representatives, reading literature, or comparing broad price quotations. It is also very difficult to get comparable cost data from various vendors. A good RFP will force a vendor to detail costs in such a fashion as to make comparison possible, i.e. for specific configuration. Make sure you are comparing apples to apples. This is where you take your analysis and operational it into a description of your dream system. It is necessary to take the data you have gathered and break it into functional specifications and technical specifications. Functional specifications describe the capabilities that you want in a system. Technical specifications deal with standards that must be adhered to guarantee minimum system performance.

Tasks

* Write narrative to describe the Library System including statistical description of users, their use of services, community growth, projected five-year growth of demand for library services.
* Write functional specifications for a system.
* Write technical specifications for a system.
* Develop criteria by which proposals will be analyzed and evaluated.
* Distribute RFP to appropriate vendors of automated systems.

2.1.8 Analyze proposals and select vendor

To analyze vendor responses to RFP and to select a vendor to implement a system.

Tasks

* Evaluate vendor proposals.
* Draft interview questions for vendor supplied contacts.
* Call Vendor references and interview them.
* Select top two or three proposals.
* Arrange for Vendor onsite demonstrations/ presentations.
* Have selection committee make site visits to systems that have actually implemented systems from top vendors and ask them to talk about their experience working with the vendor.
* Draft a list of questions to ask each vendor during the presentation.
* Analyze results of presentations/demonstrations.

For presentation

* Request that high priority modules be demonstrated first.
* Request the display of a tagged full MARC record.
* Ask if the version that is being demonstrated for each module is the same as the version in current release, i.e. what you would be getting if you bought the system today.
* Watch for cumbersome or awkward operations within or between functions.

In addition to the canned demo, ask that specific searches, operations, be performed that are analogous to real situations in your library. Ask each vendor to perform the same operations.

2.1.9 Begin contract negotiation with top vendor

To purchase a library automation system. Purpose is to

interpret and clarify the differences between a vendor's response and the library's specifications, to formalize pricing and payment schedules, deal with nonperformance issues and remedies as well as warranties, vendor bankruptcy, software infringement, and maintenance expectations. Safeguards conformance to any legal requirements necessitated by the library's parent organization or governing board.

Tasks

* Involve legal counsel, together with library personnel, in drafting or evaluating a contract.
* Compare list of necessary contract elements to actual contract.
* Reference RFP in contract.
* Set up a Contract Negotiation Agenda.
* Bring negotiations to a successful and favorable conclusion.

2.1.10 Project administrations and staffing

Library automation succeeds through the work performed by hardware, software, and people. Without the right human skills, no matter how advanced the technological tools, library automation will yield disappointing results. The person who establishes the plan needs to have a vision that extends beyond the tasks of identifying and selecting a system. All organizations need someone on the library staff who grasps the full scope of the organization's mission, operational resources, and constraints. Staying within the library cannot learn this. This person must spend 50% of his or her time outside the department, building peer relationships with IT, management or any other department working with information resources.

The primary activity of the visionary is to discover what goals and resources the library currently, and potentially shares with the other groups. With the vision established, you can focus on the unique skills, expertise and resources the library has to offer. This is a good basis for building cooperation among the groups. A library, by any definition, exists to provide economy in sharing of information resources, traditionally books and journals. But the scope of resources is ever expanding, especially in special libraries. A person who works with other groups in planning for automation must look for needs that can be filled by his or her department. Take this planning phase as an opportunity to share expertise and educate other groups about the expertise you can offer. Information content management skills are lacking throughout all organizations. This is a library's opportunity to assert its place in information content management. A person with special competency, personal and professional, should be assigned to this role.

Once the project for implementing an integrated automation solution is defined, accepted and moving forward, the visionary/coordinator often continues as the project manager. Additionally, with the right technical expertise, that person may also be given the responsibility of handling networking, hardware, and operating system issues.

Where does the expertise originate for the roles described? It comes from having a solid grounding in several areas that aren't necessarily part of a single degree program. The following types of courses are crucial for a database administrator: systems analysis, fundamentals of computing, database management systems (addresses the types, range, and tools that are available), organizational structures, cataloging and indexing theory, and thesaurus development. Hands on experience doing reference/research work, plus indexing experience will give the person realistic understanding of the challenges of building a database of quality, and the tools needed to do it efficiently.

Where does one find courses or continuing education to acquire this expertise? Not many schools offer them all; many of the best have closed in past years. The teaching staff is not there to sustain a program that addresses this multi-disciplinary field. Visit schools of information and library science, computer science, and business and describe what you are seeking. We can only hope that if the requests come frequently enough, especially in this age of knowledge management, higher education will begin to respond.

2.1.11 Upgrade and expansion plans

Before finalizing the proposal its keep in mind that the current system should be upgrade and expanded as required.

2.1.12 Timeline

Create a Timeline and try to stick to it. This Timeline should include:

* Weeding (as much time as needed probably 6 months for small collection)
* Automation system selection (insure as many of your staff as possible have input of the selection)
* Retrospective conversion from paper to electronic using a vendor (most vendors want 6 weeks to complete the conversion project.)
* Bar-coding the collection (This can be done in conjunction with Retrospective Conversion.)
* Selecting the computer hardware needed and ordering the hardware or getting bids (this may be part of selecting the automation system).
* Installing the hardware and library automation software.

2.1.13 Training staff

A vital step in the installation of a new library system is ensuring that all library staff members are comfortable with the new system's operation before it goes live. A well-trained staff member is not only more competence and control to library users. Training has many facets. Your goal should be not only to instruct your staff which key to push at what time, but also to interpret your library's policies as they are represented by your new library system software. Reaching this goal may involve revisiting your library mission and goals statement, which may very well change in view of your new library system.

2.1.14 Budget

How much money do you have or need? This will depend on the size of your collection and the potential growth expected. If you have professional librarians and lots of skilled staff then one of the larger library automation systems may be what you need.

If you have a collection of no more than 40,000 titles and expect minimal growth in the next 3 to 5 years, then one of the smaller less expensive systems could fit your needs.

If funding is available, hiring an Automation Consultant could be one of the best decisions you make.

2.1.15 Turnkey systems

Turnkey system means just turns the key and system automatic operates. But in the library science parlance, turnkey system is a complete packaged of library software and related hardware, installed by a vendor on the library and fully operational. In this system a library issued a complete order for one vendor for hardware, software, training, installations, warrantee etc and the vendor of turnkey system is responsible for dealing with any problems in the system.

2.2 Implementation

The implementation of any new system of any new system in any library is very challenging task It's varies according to library planning, preference ad the nature of the library software and hardware. The following library implementation plans may be considered in a standard library.

2.1.1 Transition process

After successfully designing of the system, the physical components are placed in their operational stage. This stage consists of two steps, implementation and evaluation. Implementation is the process of putting the new equipment to use, train the users, install the new application and construct the data file required. The most important work in implementation is the system conversion. It is the process of changing from the old system to new one. There are following method to convert the old system to new one.

* **Direct conversion :** Complete conversion of old library system to a new system with a sort period. It's a very risky because no other alternative system to fall back, if any serious problems arise.
* **Parallel conversion :** Both existing and new system is operated parallel. It's a costlier but safest conversion.
* **Phased conversion :** When the automation is not possible to install at once, then select the phased wise automation.
* **Pilot conversion :** When the new system involves in new techniques, then pilot conversion may be preferred.

There are three central elements to a successful transition:

* Retrospective conversion for books, the databases have been created in MARC format.
* Convert Patrons file or create patrons database.
* Training of staff for new procedure.

2.2.2 Benchmark test

Benchmark test is typically conducted after a vendor has been selected but before the system is actually installed in the library and prior to any payments by the library to the vendor. A Benchmark test may be necessary if the system being proposed exceeds the capabilities of any of the vendor's systems that are currently installed. Benchmark tests require careful planning and preparation and should be devised with legal counsel. A detailed "script" of transactions to be performed at each terminal should attempt to reflect the library's "real" operating environment.

Benchmark tests are costly and time consuming and should not be automatically required of every vendor responding to the RFP.

Benchmark is a latest term and very useful test for big

library, details about the benchmarking is given in next page. (2.4)

2.2.3 Performance test

The library as an alternative to, or in conjunction may require a Performance bond with a benchmark test. Performance bonds require that the vendor place a specified amount of money with a third party until the system has been installed and accepted by the library. The performance bond needs to be incorporated and fully described in the RFP.

Typical Performance Tests

* **System Reliability Test:** confirms that the system is fully operational for the percentage of time that has been specified in the RFP.
* **Functional performance acceptance tests:** simply verify that the system capability can perform according to the functional requirements set out in the RFP and in the system's documentation.
* **Full-load response time test :** Determines whether the system can perform within required response-time tolerances under a full transaction load. the maximum response times required by the library will have to be carefully detailed in the RFP. The vendor and the library together usually develop the testing of the system during the contract negotiation and these tests result expectations are incorporated into the contract. Usually extend from 60 to 90 days after the library's bibliographic and patron databases have been loaded. These types of tests should never be performed with test data supplied by the vendor.

2.2.4 Contract negotiations

It is a library responsibility to negotiate the terms of the contract for purchase of library automation products and services in to protect the interests of the library and its patrons. It must be clearly mentioned in RFP. Generally the following clause should me mentioned:

* Know the proper roles of each individual involved such as library's representative, Library administration, and Sales representative from Vendor Company, Lawyer representing the library, and lawyer representing the vendor.
* The vendor is responsible for delivering automated systems.
* The warranty period
* Payment terms
* Damaged clause
* Statuary taxes

2.2.5 Contract agreement

The agreement during the negotiations should spell out in written format.

Vendor responsibilities

i. The vendor is responsible for supplying automated systems that perform at the time of demonstration and mentioned in its technical documents.

ii. The vendor is responsible to solved the problem in proper time

iii. The vendor provide the technical and operating support to successful implementation and ongoing maintenance of the system.

iv. Proper training is provided by the vendor.

v. Systems upgrade.

vi. Compatibility of component and operation.

vii. Testing and reporting

viii. Payment of any taxes.

ix. Site preparation.

x. Provide documentation.

Library responsibilities

i. Providing staff, specified in terms of qualification and times of availability.

ii. Site preparation with the help of vendor.

iii. To check the installed system properly.

iv. Obtain the testing report.

v. Payment the outstaying payment of vendor after proper checking.

vi. Select the conversion procedure.

vii. Validation the database.

System specification: Hardware and software: A computer operating system in the underlying software that is usually provided by the hardware manufacturer from whom you purchased your system. Arguments outlining advantages and disadvantages of operating systems are beyond the scope of this document. Most library system vendors offer software that runs on more than one operating system platform.

2.2.6 Procurement method

Library should determine the portal process as per RFP in a fair way.

2.2.7 Retrospective conversion

Retrospective conversion is the a process of turning a library's existing paper catalog records into machine-readable (MARC standard) form. Retrospective conversion usually entails using shelf list cards and sometimes cards from the public catalog to find matching bibliographic records in a database of machine-readable records, and bringing those records into the existing local database. The process of locating matching records and bringing them into the local online catalog can be done in-house or it can be outsourced to a vendor that specializes in doing such work for a library.

2.2.8 Training of patrons and staff

Many vendors offer systems training as part of the system purchase and installation package, including it in the purchase price. Others make it available for additional cost. Also, most vendors make available their training curricula and visual aids for your use in local training efforts.

In addition, may vendor's offer follow-up training several weeks or months after your system has gone live in order to show advanced capabilities or specific training issues that arise after installation.

What kinds of training facilities are desirable?

The optimal training facility is a well-lighted, well-ventilated room with a number of wired workstations. The room should be able to be darkened for demonstrations by the instructor using a computer projector. Workstations should be Internet accessible and should have appropriate browser and/or client software installed. The trainer should be able to project images onto a screen visible to all participants.

How does your staff training currently take place?

Many larger libraries have adopted the "train the trainer" model. With this model, motivated and articulate library staff members are identified as leaders with the responsibility of training other staff. These training leaders are given comprehensive training by the library systems vendor, who supplies them with visual aids and a training curriculum. Once trained, the leaders hold training for smaller subgroups within the library system until everyone has been trained.

Your vendor will advise you as to the types of training classes that they offer, the optimum class size, and the duration of each applications training session. Your library may want to consider closing the library for a day to ensure that everyone is trained on the new system.

How computer literate is your staff?

This is not a silly question. Some veteran library staff members are not comfortable in a Graphical User Interface (GUI) or Windows environment or with handling a mouse for input. If you're migrating from a "legacy" system that was text-based, those staff members will need to learn an entirely different skill set before they can make most efficient use of a GUI-based application. We strongly recommend that any staff member that is not mouse/GUI competent be trained on those skills before you attempt to train them on any library system software. You may encounter some resistance and even attrition from employees who are not comfortable with these new demands. This is perfectly normal.

2.2.9 Other consideration

Technology currently in the library and its user. Other sources of technology such as the RFID and Digital library. Type of Internet access currently available at your library, any plans for changes and associated cost ex. Z39.50.

How patrons and other libraries will access your automated system from outside the library and/or how you plan to continue to meet your resource sharing commitment to other libraries. On going source of MARC records for your database and associated cost. Ex. OCLC database

2.3 Evaluation

The evaluation of library automation system should be evaluated in following sub-systems:

2.3.1 Cataloguing

* The vendor ensures that the product is fully MARC 21 compliant - that all bibliographic and authority records comply completely with Library of Congress MARC 21 format and must follow the AACR2 cataloging rules.
* The system must include built-in default templates for all valid MARC 21 material types. The user must be able to modify these templates without a programmer's assistance.
* The length of the fields for the MARC record must be determined by MARC 21 standards and not by the vendor. Provide the lengths of fields where they differ from the MARC 21 standard.
* Repeatable fields are accommodated where they conform to MARC 21 standards. Explain any limits on repeatable fields established by the vendor rather than MARC 21.

* Batch adding, editing and deleting of MARC 21 tags and subfields, other data field and call number punctuation must be possible.
* It must be possible to insert diacritics in any MARC 21 bibliographic record.
* Issues of a serial (as well as volumes of multi-volume sets and copies of a title) have copy records attached to a single bibliographic record. Individual issues and volumes do not appear in the OPAC.
* The librarian has the ability to define an unlimited number of circulation types.
* He is able to assign a different circulation type to different copies of the same title.
* He must be able to delete copy information, leaving the MARC 21 bibliographic record intact.
* MARC 21 authority records are supported. List the fields, which have authority control.
* MARC 21 authority records may be created, imported, exported, edited individually or globally. Batch checking is possible. Explain the ranges.
* The system must allow for any combination of the following subject schemes: Library of Congress, Sears, and locally defined subject headings.
* There is an online guide to MARC 21 format.
* The system offers MARC 21 validation.
* There is detection of other cataloguing errors.
* The cataloging function must be fully password protected.
* The librarian must be able to rebuild indexes.

2.3.2 Barcode labels, scanners and spine labels

* The system must utilize industry standard, photocomposed or laser generated barcode labels of 14 characters (Code 39).

* The vendor must offer a laser scanner, stand and an extension cord for the scanner of at least 20 feet long. The vendor warrants these products against defects in materials and workmanship for a period of three (3) years from the date of original delivery.
* The scanner is able to function under neon interior lighting. It is able to read all industry standard barcode labels. List all available symbiosis.
* The scanner can be easily moved from the circulation workstation to the librarian's cataloguing workstation.
* The system is able to print out spine labels using a laser printer. Explain the extent to which spine labels may be customized.

2.3.3 OPAC

* Describe which of the MARC fields are indexed by the software and may be searched.
* Describe fields that are not indexed but which are searched.
* The 856 fields provide a live URL or leads to a prompt for the initiation of a web browser.
* The OPAC is multimedia - providing access not only to the web but also to audio, graphics and video clips stored locally.
* There is a bulletin board accessible from the OPAC.
* Messages may be attached to patron or material records.
* There is context-sensitive online help in all modules.
* The patron is able to place holds from the OPAC - on the next available copy of the title.
* The patron is able to access her circulation information from the OPAC including holds and checkouts.

2.3.4 Search and display

* Simple and advanced searching is supported with at least three search terms possible in advanced searching (specify the exact number).

* Boolean searching is possible.
* Phrase searching is possible.
* There is hyper search capability on subject, notes and author fields.
* All indexes may be browsed. Or specify which.
* "See" and "see also" references are supported.
* Shelf browsing is possible through call number index.
* Truncation and wildcard searching is possible.
* Searches may be limited by date, document type, or language.
* Search histories may be retrieved.
* Searches may be limited by date or call number ranges.
* Search results may be sorted.
* Bibliographies: user creates, edits, sorts, prints and saves to disk.
* The OPAC displays date of return of items on loan.
* The OPAC display the number of holds on an item.

2.3.5 Web OPAC

* Context sensitive online help
* Truncation
* MARC display
* Shelf list browse
* Executes previous searches
* Holds
* ILL
* Hyper linking of author, subject and keywords

2.3.6 Circulation

* Self-checkout is accommodated by the system. Students are able to checkout items without viewing one another's patron records. They are unable to override due dates. They do not have access to other modules of the program.

Unauthorized entry into circulation functions is ensured through the use of passwords.

* The Circulation software may be mounted on the same client as the OPAC so that students are able to switch from one to the other.
* The system must allow an authorized operator to assign loan periods, grace periods, and fine amounts for different types of patrons and items.
* Ability to set loan policy by circulation type for each patron type.
* Ability to set the number of renewals by circulation type for each patron type.
* The system must allow the librarian to set a maximum number of checkouts for each patron type that will result in a block condition during checkout. An authorized operator using an optional password must be able to override this block.
* Ability to set a maximum number of overdue for each patron type that will result in a block condition during checkout. Only authorized operator can overwrite the block.
* The system must track the last patron who had the item out prior to being checked in as lost.
* Hourly loans.
* Zero loan periods.
* Global changes may be made to patron records.
* Borrower cards may be created.
* The order of holds may be shuffled.
* Patron records and item records are created on the fly from the circulation module.
* The system must display all copies attached to a title record during a title search and allow selection of any available copy for checkout.

* The patron's card expiration date and card issue date should be apparent on the circulation screen.

2.3.7 Reports

* Reports may be exported to a word processor and edited.
* Ability to print patron notices for overdue and ready holds.
* The system must generate mailing notices that can be used with an industry standard envelope with no added user interface.
* Ability to generate list of transactions for a single patron, including current checkouts, overdue, fines owed, and hold information.
* The system is able to provide a month-by-month breakdown of usage statistics.
* The system is able to report on books on order.
* Patron and item activity reports are available.
* Ability to print statistics for user-defined LC call number ranges.
* Copies without call numbers are reported.
* Titles without copies are reported.
* The system is able to print due date slips.

2.3.8 Inventory

* The system is able to do inventory on the whole collection or part of the collection. The system is still operational while inventory is being done, with circulating items automatically being counted in inventory.
* Inventory feature must indicate number of copies inventoried as well as number remaining uncounted.
* The system must automatically reset inventory markers to initialize the inventory process.
* Ability to finalize inventories automatically and set all uncounted items to a status of Missing. The system must also indicate the year the item was missing.

2.3.9 Technical support

* Is all technical support calls are answered immediately by a technical support representative? If not, how long to customers ordinarily wait for a call back from a technician?
* What is the ration of technical support personnel on duty to customer's ratio?
* What percentages of your technicians who provide direct technical support have library science degrees?

2.3.10 Systems requirements

* The vendor will provide a complete system that includes software, comprehensive documentation, a barcode scanner and labels, software support and maintenance, training and user group support.
* The software must include integrated searching (OPAC), a web PAC, circulation, cataloging, reporting, spine label printing, and inventory programs in one package. The system must be fully integrated, with all modules sharing a common bibliographic and patron database and a common command language.
* The system must support dynamic file allocation, material records and patron records.
* The software should support TCP/IP and the Z39.50 protocol.
* The system must be Windows-based with a full graphical user interface designed to run on Windows.
* The software should use Client/Server architecture.
* The network version must be fully compatible and run on the Windows NT operating system.
* The system must be multi-tasking when operating in a networked environment (circulation and cataloguing activities should be able to take place simultaneously at different workstations).

* The system must allow every networked workstation to be used for searching (OPAC) and all other functions, including circulation.
* Where different modules are being used simultaneously on one workstation, numerous windows should be able to be opened simultaneously.
* The network version of the system must be able to support an unlimited number of workstations within a school/building site at no additional cost.
* The system must not require specialized in-house maintenance, operating personnel, or network engineers. Any librarian must be able to install all required software with the assistance of the vendor's toll free technical support.
* The program must provide the ability to back up and restore the system using floppy disk or with the assistance of a tape backup utility.

2.4 Benchmarking

History of Benchmarking in Library: In 1993, Holly Muir, a young reference librarian, lost her job when her employing corporation downsized. She decided to start her own business, identified a need, and put her ideas to work by founding Library Benchmarking International. With business plan in hand, she wrote 5 books to guide librarians through the benchmarking process, started a newsletter for corporate librarians and other interested in improving their operations, and began conducting workshops.

Definition: "Benchmarking is a Total Quality tool used to measure and compare your library's work processes with those in other libraries. The goal of benchmarking is to increase your library's performance by adopting the best practices of your library benchmarking partners. Since best library practices are always evolving, benchmarking should be applied at least annually".

So we can say that benchmarking comes out of total

quality and is to make or improve your library's service or product better meet the needs of your customers. Keep in mind that this not only includes library customer. In the parlance of library and information science the TQ means full satisfaction to library's customers.

What to benchmark

* *Library resources*: Throughout time, libraries have been associated with the resources they hold.
* *Library processes*: Any service or function in the library that takes certain inputs, acts upon them & produces an output.

Benchmarking benefits : Find out what benchmarking can do for the library and library staff?

* *Improves your library's performance*: It can help you improve your library to better meet the needs of your customers and to make it operate more efficiently and effectively. By identifying best practices you can maximize your current resources. It also can be used to explore a new service or product that a library may want to adopt.
* *Gains/Improves upper management support*: It can be used to help you gain or improve the support of upper management. The thinking behind this is that benchmarking makes you look more proactive, demonstrates that you can operate like a business and shows that the library is solving its own problems with the good of the organization in mind. It makes the library look more like a team player which may protect its budget in the long term or even gain increased resources.
* *Builds professional relationships*: It helps build relationships within the organization and profession. And these types of relationships can be very helpful after the benchmarking study is completed.
* *Meets strategic goals*: Benchmarking can support corporate, organization or library goals. If the company

wants to cut costs, the library can look for ways to help the company or even cut library costs. A benchmarking study can help showcase the library process that is selected for benchmarking or can show why other processes are not selected.

* *Proves your library's value*: Benchmarking can help show how valuable library resources and staffs are to the company.

Benchmarking process: Why would you want to benchmark a library work process instead of the number or type of library resources?

* *Benchmark libraries in different environment*: first of all benchmarking work processes allows you to benchmark with libraries in different environments. While the resources may be different in libraries, the processes used purchase and process them may be the same. For years libraries have claimed to be unique because their collections were different. Libraries share more similarities via processes than differences.
* *Tells you how to improve*: Benchmarking a library process identifies the how to improve. Let's look at journals. Benchmarking the journal collections in two libraries can show how many each have, how often their used, what titles each library has, etc. But that won't tell you how to improve collection development or routing services. Your library partner could have more journals, but that doesn't mean they have a better journal routing procedure.
* *Explains why you need librarians*: benchmarking explains the need for the library staff. The library is not just a collection of materials, it is a service run by living human beings. Benchmarking library work processes explains to upper management and to customers what those human beings in the library do, how well they are doing it, and how they can do it better with beneficial results.

* *Uses 'business approach*: And last, benchmarking is a valid tool used by leading corporations with measurable results. Libraries can be operated more like a business, and the willingness of librarians and staff to employ benchmarking to measure and improve their products and services will usually be met with support.

2.5 Library System Request for Proposals (RFP)

The Library is soliciting written quotations from qualified vendors to for the purchase and installation of an integrated online library system.

Listed below are the specifications for the system. If the proposed software program does not fully comply with any one of these requirements, the vendor is requested to address each deviation in writing; describing how the proposed product differs. If it is felt that the specified requirement is not meaningful or critical, the vendor should note this and provide a rationale for this understanding.

The vendor is requested to submit the following to Library:

1. Terms of proposal
   * Pricing options
   * Copies of any license agreements, purchase agreements, maintenance agreements or other agreements provided by the vendor.
   * Proposal Validity Period
   * Withdrawal of Proposals
   * Proposal Rejection
   * Vendor's Cost to Develop Proposal
   * News Releases
   * Warranties
   * Contract Documents
   * Proposal Evaluation
   * System Capacity Requirements

2. Form of proposal
   * Cover Letter
   * Vendor Profile
   * Customer References
   * Configurations and Costs
   * Contract and License Terms
   * Response to Specifications
   * Other Information
3. General system requirements
   * System Architecture
   * Software
   * Hardware
   * RDBMS / Applications / Database Management
   * Industry Standards / Protocols
   * Security / Access Control
   * Services
4. Software functional requirements
   * Bibliographic Control / Cataloging
   * Authority Control
   * Circulation
   * OPAC / Web Portal / Electronic Library
   * Web Portal / Context Management Solution
   * Acquisitions and Fund Accounting
   * Serials Check-in and Control
   * Reports
   * Digital Media Archive

Chapter 3
Library Software and Hardware

3.1 Library Software

The success of library automation systems are depending upon the features of software application. A large number of software is available today's to automate the library. But the question is that, whether a librarian should go for a library package. Most popular Indian and International software are given below.

3.2 Indian Software

Most popular Indian Library Software are given below:

3.2.1 SOUL (Software for University Libraries)

INFLIBNET Center has developed Windows based Library Management Software "SOUL", which provides total solution for Library Automation. SOUL is designed using Client-Server Architecture which imparts extra strength to storage capacity, multiple access to single database, various levels of security, back up and storage facilities etc. It has MS-SQL Server 6.5 RDBMS as the back end. The software comprises following modules.

* Acquisition
* Catalogue
* Circulation
* OPAC
* Serial Control
* Administration

The in-built network feature of the software will allow multiple libraries of the same university to function together as well as access to the distributed databases installed at various university libraries and union catalogue mounted at INFLIBNET using VSAT network.

Acquisition

The Acquisition module enables library staff to handle the following major functions related to acquisition of library material.

* Suggestions management.
* Ordering cancellation and reminders.
* Receiving.
* Payment including fund control.
* Master file management such as currency table, vendors, publisher, user etc.

Through this module library staff can search the entire database of library holdings for the purpose of duplicate check etc. Using various combinations, number of reports could be generated.

Catalogue

This module is used for technical processing of books received from Acquisition Section, printing a range of records for verification, searching by title and accession numbers, authority files for publishers etc. One of the unique features of SOUL is accessing to authority files on screen as well as selection box in various fields of records. Once the proposed VSAT Network by INFLIBNET is commissioned this module will take care of automatic replication of data into union catalogue. This will avoid exchange of library data on physical media i.e. floppy, tape etc. This module covers following functions.

* Cataloguing Process.
* Catalogue Search.
* User Services.
* Catalogue card generation.
* Authority file maintenance.

* Retro conversion.
* Stock verification.
* Report Generation.
* Union database maintenance (local level).
* Export/Import of records.

Circulation

This module covering from membership management to maintenance of status of library items. The circulation transactions viz. issue, return, renewal, reserve, recall, hold can be successfully done Inter library loan, searching the status of every member or library item is possible. Reminders for overdue material, generation of various reports have also been covered.

OPAC

The On-line Public Access Catalogue (OPAC) of SOUL is a window to the library collection. Using the user-friendly menus, user can search for an item available in the library by author, title, corporate author, conference name, subject descriptors, class number etc. The Boolean search enables the user to conduct the search using all combinations including type of material, language, year etc. Besides, this will serve as first point of information about the library and also gateway for accessing INTERNET, union databases, or any other external sources.

Serial control

The complex job of keeping track of serials can easily and effectively be handled using SOUL through its Serial Control module. This module broadly handles following functions.

* Suggestions.
* Subscription (renewal and new subscription).
* Payment including fund control etc.
* Check in of issues including prediction of issues arrival.

* Reminder generation.
* Binding management.
* Search status of every item.
* Master database management.
* Reports generation etc.

Administration

User administration facility in this module is used for creating new users and giving them right for accessing different modules.

Benefits of using SOUL

* Available at nominal cost to university libraries.
* Software designed and developed exclusively to work under university environment.
* Network feature of the software will allow multiple libraries of university to function together.
* Exhaustive training at INFLIBNET supported by comprehensive manual.
* On-site training.
* Free updating/modification.
* Free technical assistance.
* Follows INFLIBNETs recommended standards and formats such as CCF, AACR2, LCSH.

Minimum Requirements for Hardware and Software

Server

* Pentium @233 MHz with 64 MB RAM
* 1.2 GB HDD
* 32 x CDROM Drive
* 1.44" Floppy Drive
* Colour Monitor (SVGA)
* Windows-NT Operating System

* MS-SQL Server 6.5

Client

* Pentium @233 MHz with 32 MB RAM
* 1.2 GB HDD with 10 MB Free space
* 1.44" Floppy Drive
* Colour Monitor (SVGA)

  Windows-95 Operating System +

3.2.2 LibSys

LibSys for library automation is the prime mission of New Delhi based software company-Info Tek Consultants Pvt. Ltd. Head Office in Gurgaon, India.

Presently LibSys is available as two products:

LibSys4 : A standard product with full-fledged functionalities as usually required in universities, large academic institution, special libraries, public libraries, etc.

LSEase : A downsized product derived form LibSys4 for corporate, colleges and school libraries where some special functionality may not be required.

Both LibSys4 and LSEase can be implemented in Client Server mode providing complete range of features expected from any advanced library system.

The integrated systems consisting Acquisition, Cataloguing, Circulation, Serials Control and OPAC modules. In LibSys a special option of 'Add on' facilities are available in the standard LibSys 4 and LSEase:-

LSWeb OPAC: Making available OPAC on a browser on Internet or Intranet.

LSWeb Client: To run the entire Libsys4/LSEase through a web browser.

LSMirroring: Enables maintaining a mirror image of LibSys database on other Server machine.

LSUnicode: Unicode support on various languages/ scripts.

Lsmart: For self check-out, book drop etc. in a security system.

Contact Address: LibSys Corporation
633-A, Phase-V, Udyog Vihar,
Gurgaon-120016 (Haryana)
INDIA
e-mail:info@libsys.co.in

3.2.3 Rovan LMS

Rovan LMS is the product of Rovan Technologies, the leading company in Sivakasi, India. Rovan LMS, the state of the art library management system helps the librarians manage the resources effectively and provide improved services to the members. ROVA LMS is suitable for school, college public and business libraries. Three editions and all are priced nominally.

* Rovan LMS Gold
* Rovan LMS Silver
* Rovan LMS Bronze

Contact address: Rovan Technologies
196 Palaniandavarpuram Colony,
Sivakasi-626189 Tamil Nadu, India

3.2.4 Libsuite

Libsuite is a ISO 9001-2000 company, located in India in the city of Pune. It supports various operations of library like Cataloguing, Circulation, Serial Control, Budgeting, and OPAC. It support digital library functionalities with multimedia file attachments etc. It works with various backend like Oracle, SQL Server, Sybase and is also available with MA ACCESS for smaller databases.

3.2.5 Autolib

AutoLib provide total Library Automation Solution at a very nominalv cost. It has been designed, and promoted by M/S Auto Lib Software Systems.

Minimum Hardware Requirements

Server : Pentium III with 64/128 MB RAM, 10/20 GB HD, FDD/CD-ROM/SVGA Monitor/LAN card and other accessories

OS : Windows NT 4.0 or Windows 2000 server NODES Pentium II/III/Celeron, 32/64MB RAM/4GB HD, monitor LAN card and other accessories

OS : Windows 95/98/workstation/2000 professionals

Contact Address: AutoLib Software Systems

B2-Solai Apartments (Opp.to MGR Garden)

Mount -Poonamallee Road

Ramapuram

Chennai 600 089, T.N, INDIA

Web: http://www.autolib-india.net/www.autolib-india.com

Email : autolib@yahoo.com_ _autolib@vsnl.net

3.3 International Software

3.3.1 VTLS (VIRTUA)

VTLS is a leading global company that creates and provides visionary technology in library solutions. It has three distinctive divisions that provide these solutions to a diverse customer base of more than 900 libraries in over 32 countries.

* VIRTUA division remains focused on ILS solutions
* Digital Asset Creation & Management division provides cutting edge software and services for Digital Libraries. VTLS is also one of the few ISO 9001 quality certified companies within the library industry.
* VTRAX division focuses on RFID type technologies through its' partnership with Tagsys

VIRTUA

Fully integrated, Flexible and ease of use that library patrons and staff demand, Virtua lets you set the rules and parameters that work best for your library. Easy to use and easy to train, Virtua offers integrated functionality between modules, including the system's cataloguing, acquisitions, serials, circulation and reporting functions.

The following module wise features are given below:

Acquisitions objectives

It takes you step by step through the various Acquisitions workflows, from adding your first purchase order and receiving items to creating your first invoice and payment voucher.

Key features of cataloging

The Cataloging subsystem is designed to offer catalogers a sophisticated cataloging tool via a Windows-based, graphical user interface (GUI) that is seamlessly integrated with the online public access catalog. Although the Virtua MARC Cataloging Editor is fully integrated with the other Virtua subsystems, it can also operate as a standalone system.

Within the GUI environment of the MARC Editor, you can create and edit database and local records, choose to have a record masked, validate record data, import records from external vendors, convert imported records into Virtua's UTF-8 (Unicode) character set, export records to classic VTLS format, and copy catalog.

Virtua serials control

A serial is a publication in any medium issued in successive parts. The different parts are numbered or bear some other chronological designation. It is the coding of these different parts in a MARC holdings record that allows for automated serials control.

Virtua Serials Control adheres to the standard MARC 21 Format for Holdings Data and provides functionality for the following tasks:

* Creating and maintaining holdings information
* Checking in serials

* Predicting issues
* Creating routing lists
* Producing reminders
* Producing and transmitting claims
* Managing binding tasks

Virtua's circulation module

It gives you the flexibility and tools you need to keep things moving at the fast-paced circulation desk. Multiple windowing capabilities and single-click access to functions allows staff members to efficiently check-in, checkout, renew and place holds on items. Fully-featured:

* *Reserve Book Room*: Handles multiple reserve locations with varying open and closed schedules, loan periods, and loan privileges.
* *Homebound services* : Helps you reach out to patrons who don't have Internet access or can't visit the library. Virtua's Homebound Services create reading list based on the user's preferences and/or circulation history, and tracks loan history to avoid repeat delivery.
* *Self-check unit* : Patrons can checkout multiple items accurately and quickly without assistance from the library staff.
* *Interlibrary Loan* : Efficient resource sharing for networking libraries that help you integrate physical or electronic document delivery into your information service.
* *Telephone Notification and Renewal* : Allows libraries to significantly reduce their notice production cost by delivering overdue and hold pick-up notices by phone.
* Staff efficiencies, user satisfaction and faster notification may be done.
* *Materials booking* : Makes it easy for library staff and patrons to reserve library equipment, meeting rooms, and materials such as conference rooms, and course reserve materials.

Reports

Virtua's robust, web-based reporting capabilities include over 50 standard reports through Info Station. Ad Hoc reporting gives you unprecedented flexibility in managing the information in your Virtua database. This custom reporting system makes use of Oracle databases for selecting in specific query.

Virtua OPAC

The Virtua OPAC offers various key features, which help facilitate your search for library material. You can use four types of searches to search the Virtua OPAC:

* *Browse Search* : Lets you search on a term and browse, or scan, an alphanumeric list of entries in the database that come closest to matching that term. If Virtua finds no exact match for your browse search query, your search results appear as an alphanumeric list of terms that come *closest* to meeting your search criteria.
* *Heading Keyword Search* : Lets you search for words and phrases within authority headings. Unlike browse searches, which display results as an alphanumeric list of headings in the database, a heading keyword search displays only the headings that contain your search term.
* *Bibliographic Keyword Search* : Lets you search for keywords and phrases within bibliographic records. Virtua offers precision searching, which gives you enhanced control through expanded bibliographic keyword search capabilities. Precision searching lets you build complex search queries using a combination of keywords, search operators, proximity, truncation, wild cards, filtering, and more than 180 configurable keyword search categories.
* *Control Number Search* : Lets you perform a search using the unique alphanumeric identifiers that are assigned to records in the database. Control number searches give you fast, direct access to the records in your database.

Because the Virtua OPAC is seamlessly integrated with all other Virtua subsystems, you can use the client OPAC as the starting point for many of the tasks that you will perform in Virtua, including circulation control and cataloging.

VICTORS iPortal

* Reviews and rank titles in the Vectors iportal, in a very unique feature.
* Unicode standard on both the client and server levels. In the Vectors iPortal, changing the interface language is as simple as the click of a mouse. Users can view and print records in any languages.
* Fully customizable, the VICTORS iPortal reflects an image as unique as your users. The flexibility of VECTORS allows you to change the entire face of the software. Patrons can view the catalog through their preferred interface-whether that interface is designed for the advanced user, student, or child.
* Allow linking to book cover images, full electronic table of contents, published book reviews, video trailers for DVDs, and many other resources.
* Patrons can perform federated and consolidated searches to retrieve information from any Z39.50 database the library selects. Search filters and multiple sorting option allow users to view only the result they desire, in whatever order they prefer.

Digital asset creation & management

Digital Asset Management System - based on the Fedora – Open-Source Digital Object Repository Architecture Software for managing, creating, storing, indexing, cataloging, searching & retrieving your digital collections

VITAL Components

VITAL Manager

Windows 2000 and XP

Fedora™ Repository

UNIX/LINUX, SUN and Windows

VITAL Access Web Portal

UNIX/LINUX and Windows

XML Cataloging Utility

EAD, DC & MARC XML Templates

VITAL Collection Loader

Oracle Database (Optional

*** VTRAX division focuses on RFID**

FASTRAC RFID Specifications & Guidelines

PC Requirements for RFID Workstations

Any PC that supports the following Windows Operating systems will do (so you may be able to use an existing PC's or laptops):

* We require Windows 95 or later (98, ME, NT, Win 2000, XP etc.)
* An available serial DB9 port. If your PC supports USB (Win 2000, XP), then a USB to serial converter may be used in place of the DB9 serial port. We need to know if the converter will be required, if so VTLS will supply the converter.

3.3.2 Softlink Asia

The company is associated with "Softlink International" the world leader in library software and having own establishment for more than eight years with the goal to capture the Asian region of the globe.

The company's products have been designed and developed in conjunction with professional librarians, set international benchmarks for functionality, efficiency and value. It has a worldwide acceptance and is currently being used all over the world. In this dynamic world of information it follows constant upgrading enabling to meet all kinds of requirements for all ranges of libraries

It provides a combination of ease of use and powerful search tools, allowing the right access to information, both physical and electronic, either within the organization or through the Web. Softlink's Systems are configured around Microsoft industrial strength tools and technology, with the company designated as a Microsoft Certified Solution Provider.

CONTACT ADDRESS

Softlink Asia Pvt. Ltd. Sales Office: B-24B, Kalkaji, New Delhi-110019, Ph. No. 011 26233228 / 9

Works : 10 Ashoka Enclave, 2nd Floor, Ext. III, Sector35, Faridabad–121003, Haryana Phone:Faridabad:0129 2257872 / 4 / 5 Mobile: 9810410413 / 9810276697 / 9810586437 E-Mail: softasia@del3.vsnl.net.in Website: www.softlinkasia.com

3.3.3 VOYAGER

Voyager, the integrated Library Management System from Endeavor Information Systems Inc. www.endinfosys.com.

Organized into intelligent modules, Voyager includes Web-based public access, acquisitions and serials control, cataloging and authority control, circulation and course reserves, and reporting and systems administration. Voyager is highly customizable to maximize each library's workflow. Designed with a graphical user interface operating on Microsoft Windows, it is easy to learn and use, and saves time through operator efficiency. And since it's build on open systems technology, it will interoperate with existing library technology and scale to accommodate future needs.

For academic and research libraries that are faced with increasing user demands and the need to plan for the future, Endeavor's product suite provides a synthesized approach to information management and access. Voyager, ENCompass, LinkFinder*Plus*, and Meridian blend Endeavor's library expertise with the right technologies, backed by ongoing research and development. Together, they provide holistic solutions to the challenges libraries face today.

Voyager: Integrated Library System Endeavor's Integrated Library System is used by 1300 academic and research libraries around the world. Unicode compliant and feature rich, Voyager has a proven track record helping research institutions manage and provide access to their library collections.

Meridian: Electronic Resource Management System Endeavor's Meridian supports all of the administrative tasks associated with evaluating, licensing, and providing access to electronic content. It provides vital e-resource information to the library's users while alleviating the headaches of back-office management of electronic resources.

ENCompass: Digital Library System

ENCompass is Endeavor's enterprise-level system for managing and accessing content from a wide range of electronic resources, local and external. It is composed of a suite of modules, each tuned to a specific need - federated searching, building digital collections, etc. - at academic libraries and other research organizations.

3.3.4 SIRSI

Integrated Library Management Systems Integrated systems for total management

Serving library users requires a powerful, dependable information technology infrastructure. It's critical for all library operations. Open. Industry-standard. Scalable. Modular. C Sirsi offers stable, mature client/server integrated library system (ILS) technology for all types and sizes of libraries. These systems feature comprehensive ILS functionality, with modules for all public and technical services; industry-standard, scalable relational database management systems; well-defined application programming interfaces; an intuitive GUI across all modules; and a strong platform for adding new functionality to existing modules and plugging entirely new modules and clients directly into the server. Sirsi's ILS technology is also available through a convenient, cost-effective ASP service.

3.4 Open Source Software

3.4.1 CDS/ISIS

Micro CDS/ISIS is an advanced non-numerical information storage and retrieval software developed by UNESCO since 1985 to satisfy the need expressed by many institutions, especially in developing countries, to be able to streamline their information processing activities by using modern (and relatively inexpensive) technologies.

The software was originally based on the Mainframe version of CDS/ISIS, started in the late '60s, thus taking advantage of several years of experience acquired in database management software development. Several partners contributed to its development through the years.

Introduction : The major features of the CDS/ISIS software are:

* the handling of variable length records, fields and sub fields, thus saving disk space and making it possible to store greater amounts of information;
* the handling of repeatable fields;
* a data base definition component allowing the user to define the data to be processed for a particular application;
* a data entry component for entering and modifying data through user-created data base specific worksheets;
* an information retrieval component using a powerful search language providing for field-level and proximity search operators, in addition to the traditional and/or/not operators, as well as free-text searching;
* a powerful sort and report generation facility allowing the user to easily create any desired printed products, such as catalogues, indexes, directories, etc.;
* a data interchange function based on the ISO 2709 international standard used by leading data base producers;

* an integrated application programming language (CDS/ISIS Pascal and the ISIS_DLL), allowing the user to tailor the software to specific needs;
* functions allowing the user to build relational data bases, though CDS/ISIS is not based over a relational model;
* powerful hypertext functions allow to design complex user interfaces.

A Windows interface between CDS/ISIS and IDAMS, the UNESCO software for statistical analysis, has also been developed.

From the outset, CDS/ISIS was created as a multilingual software, providing integrated facilities for the development of local linguistic versions. Thus, although UNESCO distributes only the English, French and Spanish versions of the package, user-developed versions exist in virtually all languages, including special versions which UNESCO helped in developing, for Arabic, Chinese and Korean.

* Compatibility between the DOS and Windows versions No conversion is needed when moving from CDS/ISIS DOS to CDS/ISIS for Windows. However, formatting language functions are just 95% compatible. In some cases you may find some syntax errors appearing: you may have to adapt your display format to the new one. In terms of search engine, the two versions are totally compatible: both can use the same I/F (inverted file). The data entry worksheet are also compatible but the screens will appear different.
* Compatibility with different Windows versions CDS/ISIS for Windows (Winisis) is 100% compatible with all Windows Operating Systems. However Windows NT/2000/XP users should read the troubleshooting section of the "readme" file installed by the Winisis installation program. In case you get a message similar to:

"a device can attached to system is not functionning"
"cannot run 16 bit programs"

* Arabic version UNESCO and the League of the Arab States (Department of Information and library) developed an Arabic enabled version of CDS/ISIS for Windows. The latest version 1.5 runs on Win95, Win98, WinMe, 2000 and XP operating systems.

The software comes in three languages: English, Arabic (Egypt) and French. It contains as well an example database in Arabic and English.

The whole user interface is reversed Right to Left when the software starts in Arabic language. A special feature allows the switch from RTL to LTR.

3.4.2 ISIS/MARC

CDS has developed ISIS/MARC and fully supported to MARC 21 format. The format is given below:

Cataloguing procedure in WINNISIS- ISISMARC

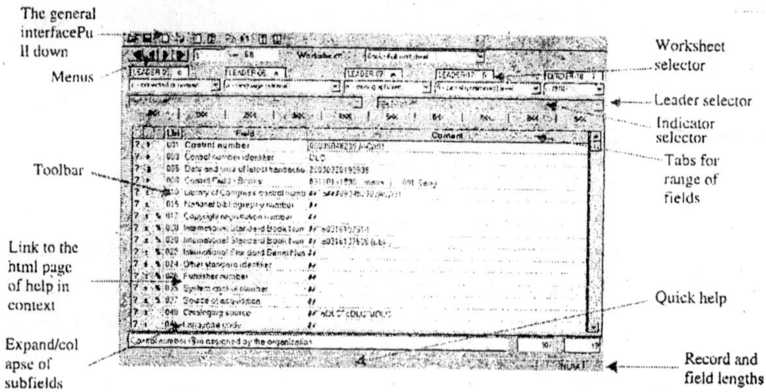

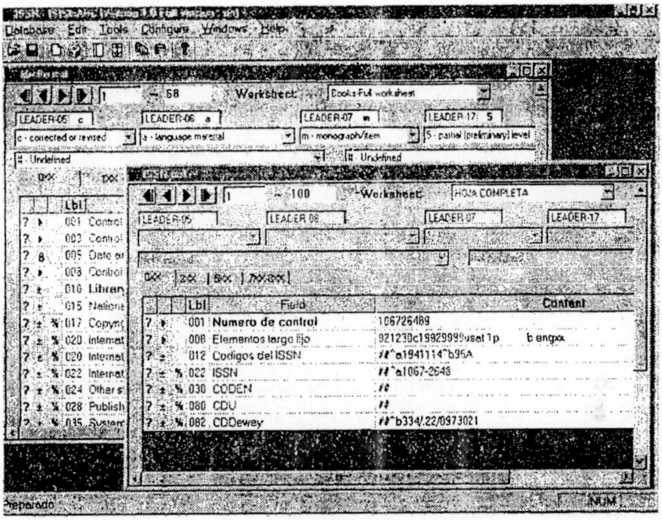

It is possible to open more than one database at the same time, to edit each one separately, to copy and paste records among the databases, etc.

In this version it not possible to open multiple instances of the same database.

Toolbar

1 2 3 4 5 6 7 8 9 10 11 12

1. Open a new database
2. Save the present record
3. Open a new record
4. Open the character map
5. View the present record with a display format
6. Toggle to display/hide unused fields in the worksheet
7. Copy record to clipboard
8. Create a record from clipboard

9. move a subfield up
10. move a subfield down
11. edit record in internal mode
12. System manual (an external file)

Icons of the dataentry worksheet

- ? Link to help page of the manual
- ▸ Manual edition
- % Repeatable field
- 🔒 Field non editable (system)
- ± Expand/collapse field in subfields
- ■ Field edited from a pick-list or an authority file

Edit menu options

The options are similar to the Winisis data entry worksheet

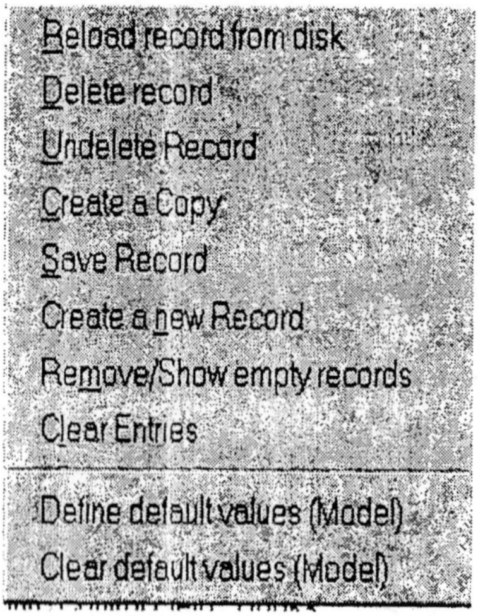

1. Load the record again from the hard disk to recover the original data.
2. Logical deletion of a record
3. Undeletion of a logical deleted record (See note[1])

4. Copy an existent record as a new one which will be the next master file number available
5. Save the record
6. Create a new record from scratch
7. Show/hide unused fields in the worksheet
8. Clean all data and present a blank record in the worksheet
9. Create a temporary worksheet with carry on data
10. Clear the temporary worksheet.

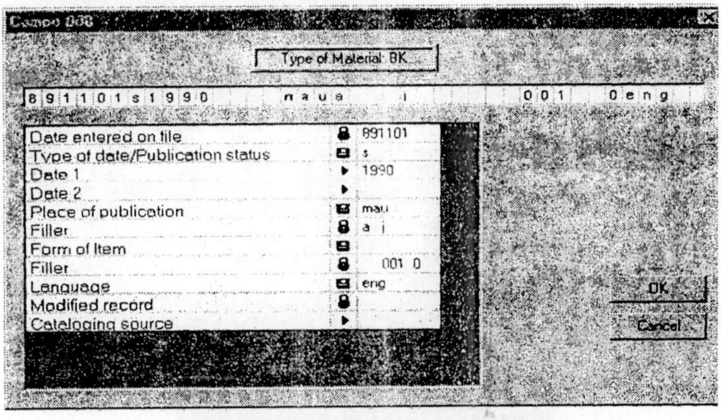

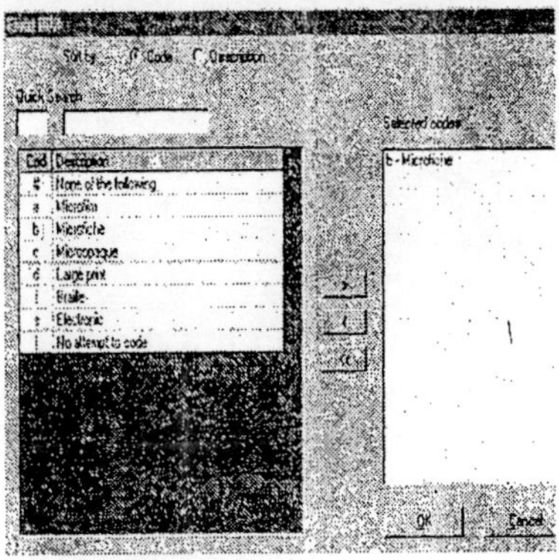

Fixed length coded fields use an special template, where each piece of the template has a predetermined number of characters and can use one of three kinds of modes for data entry.

▸	Manual edition	Free data entry
🔒	Field non editable (system)	Data is loaded using BEGIN or END commands declared in the worksheet (see)
▣	Field edited from a pick-list	Data is selected from a linked pick-list declared in the current worksheet

Any chunk of data is limited to the number of spaces assigned in the template, unused positions will be padded with either spaces or special characters declared as default in the worksheet in use.

Authority File

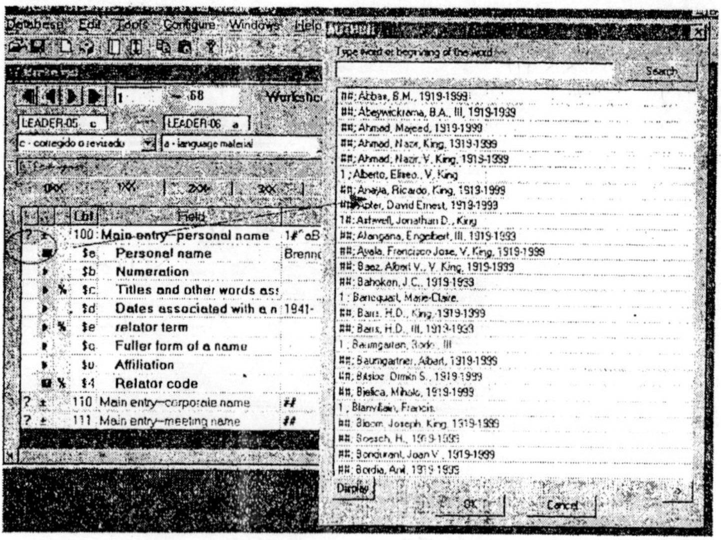

▣ ← A field linked to an authority file should link it using the first subfield of the field, and setting the attributes of this subfield with the parameters explained below in FDT21 editor.

When clicking the icon, the application will fetch the corresponding file and display in alphabetic order the entries in batch of fifties.

It is possible to type the root of a word/name to display all the entries beyond that key.

The table will display only the main entry (i.e. the standardized data), but it is possible to see the full record of the entry, clicking the button "Display" as seen below.

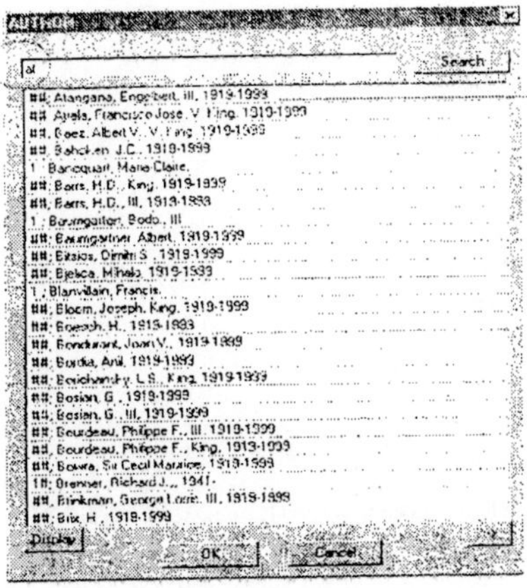

The entries in the table are displayed with indicators (in case they have it) but without subfield delimiters.

When an entry is selected the complete field of the authority file will be loaded in the field of the target database preserving the indicators and subfield delimiters (in case they have it), replacing whatever the data was present in those subfields and preserving the rest.

In case the authority file has subfields not defined in the field of the target database, those extra subfields will be eliminated in the transfer process. Authority files shouldn't be used in fixed length fields, if used the result will be impredictable.

Isismarc can handle any kind of Isis records as authority files, therefore if the records has or not has indicators or has or not has subfields, the structure will be preserved and transferred correctly.

Character map

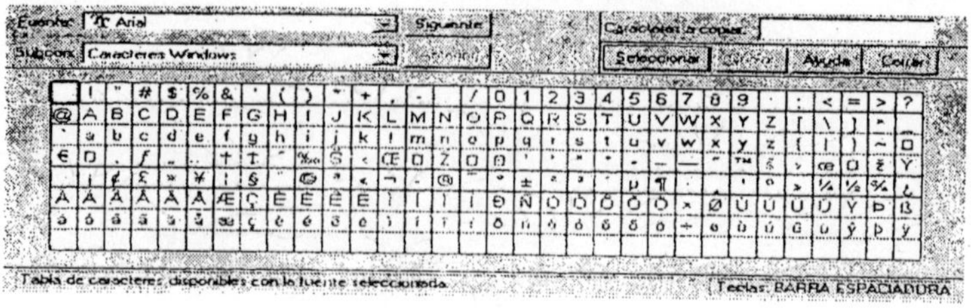

3.4.3 KOHA

Koha is the world's first free Open Source Library System. Made in New Zealand by the *Horowhenua Library Trust* and *Katipo Communications Ltd,* the Koha system is a full catalogue, opac, circulation, member management and acquisitions package. Koha was initially developed in 1999 and the first library went live in January of 2000. Koha's code has been in production since then and is continuing to move towards higher levels of functionality and standards compliance, including embracing the international records and cataloging standards MARC and Z39.50. Our development community has also grown and now includes contributors on four continents and ports in several languages.

Key features

* Simple clear interface for librarians and members (patrons) to search right from the front page.
* Customisable search - you choose which fields you want on your search forms when you set it up
* Reading lists for members - now you can find the name of that great book you read last year. NOTE: Our

librarians and customers love this, but if you have concerns about keeping this information it could be disabled. This is really useful for helping homebound users get fresh books

* Full acquisitions including budgets and pricing information (including supplier and currency conversion), being kept so that you can see what you've ordered and received - so handy at end of year and audit time.
* Simple acquisitions for the smaller library
* Able to catalogue websites as items, or have them as links to existing biblios.

This is one of the beauties of Free Software — all of the people involved have reasons to work on a Library System, by working together they've been able to create something far more useful than anything they could have done on their own, while enjoying the benefits of all the work done before.

1.5 Library Management Software and Hardware Checklist

How does your current system compare to a modern client/server library system? If you can't check off the following functions, you need to consider changing systems.

Company

* Many years of dedicated experience in serving the technological needs of libraries
* Long-term track record of profitability and steady revenue growth
* A loyal, satisfied customer base, representing libraries like yours
* No "legacy" systems - customers continue to use their original system, updated annually with the latest technological advances available

Technology

* Choice of fully-developed UNIX or NT server platforms
* Choice of RDBMS
* Scalable to any size with advanced multi-tier, client/server design
* Full-text bibliographic search engine
* Centralized software and configuration management of all desktop clients in the network
* Easy Windows Wizards for all system administration functions

Flexibility

* Simple Interview Wizards to enable easy system set-up and local customization
* Unlimited size of parameter tables
* Easy global changes for parameter tables
* Ability to easily establish additional fields
* Ability to produce statistical reports for these additional fields
* Fully documented and easy-to-use Application Program Interface (API)

Management Reports

* A variety of report templates that are easily customized to provide almost unlimited reporting capabilities
* Additional custom reporting via API or SQL
* Desktop reporting completely integrated with parameter tables
* Graphical report interface that enables point and click selection of appropriate data elements, time periods, frequencies, output devices, etc.

OPAC/Web Gateway

* Integrated OPAC and Internet access
* Ability to design your own OPAC and Web pages

* Custom OPAC profiles based on a user's login or IP address
* Choice of icons for easy searching

Digital Media Archive

* A complete system that provides an easy way to store, organize, and access your library or archive's non-book holdings
* Maintains a variety of text, audio, and video media formats
* Supports multiple metadata formats concurrently, including Dublin Core and EAD
* Simultaneous searching of all formats
* Full-text and natural language searching
* Objects stored in their native formats

Client Design

* Streamlined Windows Wizard for every library task
* Artificial intelligence guides users quickly through each process
* Choice of mouse or keyboard entry
* Server-based client profiles enable individual user profiles to be moved automatically
* from one workstation to another
* Clients are updated automatically with push technology
* Clients are easily customized to user preferences

Cataloging/Authority Control

* Z39.50 copy cataloging with automatic holdings posted to OCLC
* Easy, direct record overlay
* Automatic generation of authority headings

Acquisitions

* Divides order amounts and percentages among funds

* Pre-processing in cataloging

Serials

* Automatic generation of prediction patterns
* SICI-based checkin to the issue level

Circulation

* Windows Wizards interface for minimal staff training
* E-mail notices
* Phone notification for all notices

Academic Reserves

* Global activation and deactivation and update of materials based on instructor, course, term, or reserve desk
* Full integration with circulation and inventory functions for tracking movement from stacks to reserve location and back

Booking

* Two-year booking calendar
* Full shipping integration
* Group bookings
* User-defined shipping schedules

Outreach Services

* Management of materials delivered to library users (e.g., homebound, nursing homes, schools, prisons, etc.)
* Schedules deliveries
* Provides interest profiles
* Automatic searching and selection of materials to match user profiles
* Reading histories to avoid duplication

Accountability

* Document classification tracking

* Support for Access Restrictions (AR) and Need to Know (NTK) Restrictions
* Support for destruction tracking
* Automatic security-based clearance/classification security

Part II : Retrospective Conversion

Chapter 4
Retrospective Conversion

4.1 What is Retrospective Conversion?

Retrospective conversion is the transfer of bibliographic information typically shown on shelf list cards into a universal, computer-readable format known as MARC format. One or a combination of two basic methods typically accomplishes it: matching and extracting machine-readable records from a resource file or keying records directly into a database.

Why is it done?

To make use of existing archival descriptions, known as legacy data, in automated and networked systems without having to re-do the description work.

How is it done?

By either:

* **Scanning the exiting finding aids**

This can only be done if the existing finding aids are good quality typescript; the resulting images will need to be run through optical character recognition software to produce "live" documents which can then be imported to the automated system.

* **Re-keying the existing finding aids**

This is becoming the more usual method because it allows almost any type of exiting finding aid, including hand-written cards and lists, to be converted; also the re-keying can be done to meet standard format.

4.2 Standards for Retrospective Conversion

It is a most challenging and time taking tasks for library. So that certain guidelines should be prepared with proper standards.

4.2.1 Preparation of project specifications

Retrospective Conversion Team prepare project specifications for the project, the specifications contain detailed information and instructions on all aspects of the project, including books to be skipped, records to be flagged, and guidelines for matching and editing records and for recording location, call number, and other copy-specific information. The following information should be required for Retrospective Conversion.

4.2.2 Customizing your database

The program has default "Item Classes", i.e., Report Classes, Material Types, Circulation Types, Age Groups, and Locations. The appropriate Item Class will be chosen as items are entered into your conversion database based on how you fill out this form. You may have different categories in each item class. You may add additional sheets if necessary.

* **Report Class** : A Report Class is the Dewey Decimal classifications that are used to identify your collection of materials. A Circulation statistics report is compiled based on your choices of Report Classes. Please find listed below the Report Classes. If there are any that you do not use, please cross them out, and we will remove them, if possible. If there are others that you do use and are not listed, please fill in the blanks with the necessary information. Other Report Classes might be Reference, Big Books, Professional Materials, Equipment, Kits, or Story Collection.

Report Class	Description
000	Dewey Range 000 – 099
100	Dewey Range 100 – 199
200	Dewey Range 200 – 299
300	Dewey Range 300 – 399
400	Dewey Range 400 – 499
500	Dewey Range 500 – 599

600	Dewey Range 600 – 699
700	Dewey Range 700 – 799
800	Dewey Range 800 – 899
900	Dewey Range 900 – 999
Biography	Biographies
Fiction	Fiction
Easy books	Children's Easy books
Videocassettes	Videocassettes
Audiocassettes	Audiocassettes
Filmstrips	35mm Filmstrips
Large Print	Large Print manuscripts
____________	________________
____________	________________
____________	________________
____________	________________
____________	________________
____________	________________
____________	________________
____________	________________

* **Material Type** : A Material Type is the physical form for items in your collection. Please find listed below the Material Types. If there are any that you do not use, please cross them out and we will remove them, if possible. If there are others that you do use and are not listed, please fill in the blanks with the necessary information. Other Material Types might be Paperback Books, Books on Tape, AV Equipment, Magazines/ Periodicals, Teaching Guides, or Study Units.

Note: Please include all material types that you have in the library. If your paperback books are inter-shelved with the hardback books and you would like to know how many of your books are paperback, then you could have Paperback as a Material Type and track their statistics from here.

Material Type	Description
Language material	Includes printed, microform, and electronic language material.
Notated music	Includes microform and electronic notated music.
Cartographic material	Includes maps, atlases, globes, digital maps etc.
Projected medium	Examples include: motion pictures, video recordings
Musical recording	Examples include: compact discs, or cassette tapes.
Computer file	Includes the electronic resources: computer software
________	________________
________	________________
________	________________
________	________________

* **Bibliographic Level** : Indicates the bibliographic level of the record.

Material Level	Description
Monographic component part	A monographic bibliographic unit that is such that the retrieval of the component part is dependent on the identification and location of the host item or container.
Serial component part	A serial bibliographic unit that is physically attached to or contained in another serial unit such that the retrieval of the component part is dependent on the physical identification and location of the host item or container.

Collection	A made-up multipart group of items that were not originally published, distributed, or produced together.
Subunit	A part of a collection, especially an archival unit described collectively elsewhere in the system.
Integrating resource	A bibliographic resource that is added to or changed by means of updates that do not remain discrete and are integrated into the whole. Examples include: Updating loose-leafs and updating Web sites.
Monograph/item	An item either completes in one part or intended to be completed in a finite number of separate parts.
Serial	An item issued in successive parts bearing numerical or chronological designations and intended to be continued indefinitely.

* **Circulation Type** : The Circulation Type cross-references with the Patron Class during circulation transactions to define the way materials should circulate normally. Consider the Circulation policies that you practice and develop Circulation Types accordingly. Each Circulation Type can have a different loan period depending on who is checking out the material. For example, you only want the children/students to have "Circulation" items for one week, yet the parents/adults/teachers can have them for a longer period of time.

Please find listed below the Circulation Types. If there are any that you do not use, please cross them out and we will remove them, if possible. If there are others that you do use and are not listed, please fill in the blanks with the necessary information. Other Circulation Types might be Magazines or Equipment, or divide AV Circ into Audiocassettes, Videocassettes, etc.

Note: You will be setting circulation privileges for your patrons based on these types so be sure to include all the different loan periods that you check out the materials in your library. For example, if the loan period for audiocassettes is different from videocassettes, then they need to be given two different circulation types. If magazines are to be checked out differently from regular circulation materials, have a different circulation type for them, too. *Think of all possible types and their various loan periods.*

Circulation Type	Description
Circulation	Materials with Regular Circulation period
Reference	Reference materials
AV Circ	Audio-Visual Circulation
____________	______________________________
____________	______________________________
____________	______________________________
____________	______________________________
____________	______________________________

* **Location :** Location identifies where materials are stored in the library. If you have more than one branch, we suggest that you use each branch as a location.

Please find listed below the Locations. If there are any that you do not use, please cross them out and we will remove them, if possible. If there are others that you use and are not listed, please fill in the blanks with the necessary information. Other Locations might be a Branch Library, or other rooms in a school (Music Room, AV Closet/Room, etc.)

Note: You do not have to have more than one location; everything can be classified as Main Library. We can describe locations however is needed to meet the needs of your library.

Location	Description
Main Library	Main Library
At Circulation Desk	Items kept at the Circulation Desk

Text Book Section	Items kept at the TBC section
Reference Section	Items kept at the Reference section
Japanese Collection	Items kept at the Japanese section
____________	____________________________
____________	____________________________
____________	____________________________

4.2.3 Call number verification

The call number is the crucial part of any data conversion. A call number usually has at least two lines and is found on the spine label of the item. The Classification Number appears above the author letters. Other times there may be more lines added either above the two described above (such as Ref. or Reference) and/or below (such as c. 1or copy 1). This form is provided to help you standardize the call numbers as they are entered into your automation system. Elements of the call number need to be decided upon now.

If you have not always been the librarian at your organization, things may not be consistent. By completing this form, we can help make the appropriate changes that can make your library database consistent.

Do you want your call numbers to be all caps?

YES or NO

Do you want Collective Biography as a separate report class? **YES or NO**

If yes, you need to be sure it is listed in the "Report Class" list found on above

Do you want Reference as a separate report class?

YES or NO

If yes, you need to be sure it is listed in the "Report Class" list found on above

Do you want Paperback as a separate report class?

YES or NO

If yes, you need to be sure it is listed in the "Report Class" list found on above

In the Report Classes listed below and the following pages, please indicate the appropriate option for your local call numbers. Also indicate the corresponding material type, circulation type, age group, and location for each of the report classes listed on the following pages.

If you use a call number other than what is listed, please include a sample of that call number that shows exactly what it looks like.

Please follow the examples provided below:

Example #1 : Fiction

Call number on spine appears as:

FIC	Report class
793.73	Dewey class number
Abc	Ist 3 letters of the author's surname (book number)
Main	Location

Example #2 : Individual Biography

———B and Ist —— letters of the biographer's surname and Location

Example #3 : Collective Biography

———B and Ist —— letters of the author's surname and Location

Example #4 : Reference

______REF and Dewey # and 1st ___letters of the author's surname

Example #5 : Audiocassettes

______ AC and 1st __ letters of the title

______ AC and Classification and 1st ___ letters of the title

4.2.4 Weed your collection

This can result in a cost savings for your library and will prevent paying for records that you don't really need to have converted. These are some guidelines to expedite the weeding process:

1. Remove from the shelves materials that haven't circulated in over 5 years.
2. Remove from the shelves items that contain dated or superseded information, i.e., books on science (particularly in reference to space flight; for example, this year a man will land on the moon), computers and technology.
3. Remove from the shelves items that no longer support the curriculum and mission of your library.
4. Remove from the shelves damaged or items that cannot be repaired.
5. Remove the shelf list cards that match the items you removed from the shelves (steps 1-4 above).
6. Remove shelf list cards for materials you have declared lost or missing.

4.2.5 Arrange your self as classified order

After you have weeded your collection, read your shelves. Check your shelves for accurate description of materials and the copy and volume information. Please help us to identify multiple copies and volumes.

4.2.6 Barcodes

Do you want us to use 8-digit or 14-digit barcodes? If you do not loan your library materials to other libraries, you will probably want to use 8 digit barcodes. If you do loan your library materials to other libraries, you will probably want to use 14 digit barcodes and have the first four digits be associated with your library. The 4-digit library code can be letters or numbers. For example, Barger Academy of Fine Arts Library code could be "BAFA" or a combination of numbers such as 1234.

8 digit barcodes ______ 14 digit barcodes ______

If we use 14 digit barcodes, what 4-digit library code should we use?

Would you like to order Smart Barcodes at this time?

YES or NO

Smart barcodes would include the following information: Your library name, Title, Author, Call Number and the Human Readable Barcode number.

Top line inscription ______________________

This barcode inscription can be up to 40 characters including spaces. For

Where do I place barcode numbers?

* Place the barcode where it is easiest to scan.
* On the cover of the book (upper-left hand corner)
* On the fly-leaf inside the front cover for books
* Inside near the book pocket
* Wherever you place it, make sure it can be scanned by any automation checkout system you may purchase such as a self-check out device.

Don't forget to place book tape over the barcode to protect them. Even better, purchase laminated barcodes

4.2.7 Patron records

Patron field to be considered

* Name (first, last)
* Street Address
* Mailing Address
* Zip Code
* Telephone Number
* Social Security Number (Not required)
* Grade Level
* Notes
* Birth date
* Type of patron: Adult, Juvenile, Student, Senior

Chapter 5
Retrospective Conversion Process

5.1 Retrospective Conversions Process

Retrospective conversion can be done either shelf list card or direct book. Through shelf list card, each and every card is being matched with the external database and the record once found is downloaded to the local databases. Only call number and accession number with location gets the modified into the downloaded record. The flow chart is given below:

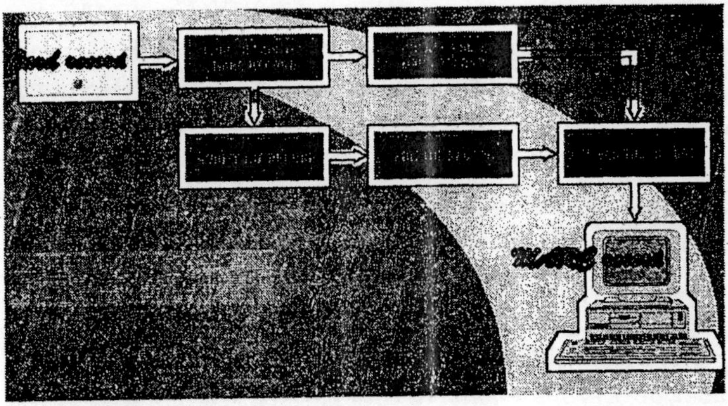

Retrospective conversion through direct book: Pick the book from stack and first matching the record from external database and if the record available in the external database, it should be matched and download in local database system after some customized like call number, accession and location etc. If the records not available in external database, create the new records as international standard with marc 21 format and save it in local database. The flow chart is given below:

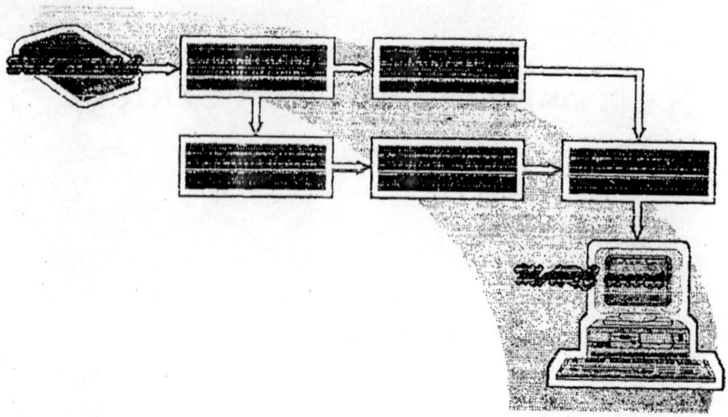

There are number of options which are available with the libraries for initiating the process of retro-conversion.

* **Direct Cataloguing:** It is a very simple option to create the bibliographic record from self-list card or books into MARC format.
* **Copy Cataloguing:** In this case shelf- list card/book is being is being matched with the external database through z3950 protocol and the record once found is downloaded to the database directly. The downloaded record can be modified as per requirement.

5.1.1 Copy cataloguing from OCLC (World Cat database) http://www.oclc.org

Retrospective conversion can be defined as the use of cataloguing information from a national bibliographic utility such as OCLC or LOC for creating online cataloguing records for older library materials. Records are edited on OCLC/LOC and exported from OCLC/LOC to our local database. For OCLC searching the following steps should be follows:

Searching OCLC

WorldCat

Window to the world's libraries

WorldCat is a worldwide union catalog created and maintained collectively by more than 9,000 member institutions. With millions of online records built from the bibliographic and ownership information of contributing libraries, it is the largest and most comprehensive database of its kind.

61 million quality records

Built by catalogers around the globe, WorldCat is the leading bibliographic database in the world, providing libraries with an extensive and rich source of cataloging records. This resource increases efficiency by ensuring a high hit rate for materials of all formats.

Bibliographic records by source of cataloging

Last revised: January 2006

Compiled from Cataloging File Statistics: Analysis of Online Bibliographic Records

Format	LC-created	Participating library records	Member -input from LC copy	Total records
Books	5,079,314	42,323,997	2,948,211	50,351,522
Serials	233,782	2,423,559	65,868	2,723,209
Visual Materials	163,078	1,776,331	28,392	1,967,801
Maps	232,252	687,249	18,307	937,806
Mixed Materials	235	265,242	860	266,337
Sound Recordings	231,064	1,761,095	57,803	2,049,962
Scores	68,381	1,204,635	53,101	1,326,117
Computer Files	7,584	246,933	878	255,395
Totals	6,015,688	50,689,041	3,173,420	59,878,149

Definition of terms

LC-created: MARC records distributed from the Library of Congress and records input directly by LC.

Participating library records: Original cataloging records input directly by OCLC members or added through Batchload.

Member-input from LC copy: Records input and transcribed from LC cataloging records.

Encoding level distribution: The distribution of values indicating the degree of completeness of the record.

Signing onto OCLC : Logging onto OCLC via Passport for Windows

* **Manoeuvring through OCLC**

F4	Page down
F5	Page up
F6	Download record to database, update record to read database
F9	Forward to next record
Shift F9	Reverse to previous record
Ctrl F9	Go back to previous index screen
F10	Send request ending where next paragraph symbol (backwards P) is located
F11	Send request ending where cursor rests when command given
Alt F11	Download record to database
Alt F12	Download record to database
Alt F3	Update record that database holds

* **Searching for a Bibliographic record**

auth, title	Use the first four letters of the author's last name, a comma, then the first four letters of the first word of the title, excluding articles (see your article list). For example, author=Robert D. Crane,

	book = *The Spirit of the West*, you would enter the search as cran,spir.
title	Use the first three letters of the first word of the title (excluding articles), a comma, the first two letters of the second word, a comma, the first two letters of the third word, a comma, and then the first letter of the fourth word. For example, book=*The Spirit of the West*, you would enter the search as spi,of,th,w.
author	Use the first four letters of the author's last name, a comma, the three first letters of the first name, a comma, and then the first letter of the middle name. For example, author=Robert D. Crane, you enter cran,rob,d.

NOTE: If the author or title does not fill the required amount of letters to do the search, it is okay, but you MUST use the cucumber of commas required for the search or the database will not know what you are looking for.

For example, author=K. Poe, book=*The Day of Delight*;

* **Additional searches**

(See your supervisor for detailed information)

OCLC control number	fin an 678987
LCCN	fin ln 72-4519
ISBN	fin bn 087793298
ISSN	fin sn 0024-2527
Gov't Docs number	fin gn gn:ga11376109
Title	fin dt xxx,xx,xx,x
Personal Name	fin dp xxxx,xxx,x
Corporate Name	fin dc xxxx,xxx,x
Author/Title	fin da xxxx,xxxx
Combined searches	fin dt xxx,xx,xx,x

and dp xxxx,xxx,
fin dt xxx,xx,xx,x
and ln 72-4519
fin ln 76-24594
and bn 0520033280

Search Qualifiers (See your	*Qualifier Codes*
Books	bks
Archives/Manuscripts	amc
Serials	ser
Computer Files	mrf
Maps	map
Musical Scores	sco
AV media	med
Sound Recordings	rec
Microform	mf
Not a microform	nm
LC	dlc
1980-1989	1980-89
1900-1999	19??
1981-1984	1981-4
1981-1992	1981-92
Up to 1981	-1981*
Since 1981	1981-*
1981	1981

Determining if record is a match:

Use the following information:

* 1XX/7XX field: Author-last name, first name or initial or corporate body
* 245 field: Title-same, however, very long titles may be shortened, and the last part may not be given, or may be represented by "...".

* 250 field: Edition-more than one edition of a book may exist, and it important to have the record which matches the edition we hold in our collection.
* 260 field: Place of publication, publisher, publication date.
* 300 field: Pagination, illustrations, size. Pagination may be off by a few pages, anything drastic is questionable.
* Other fields which can help in identification but which are not mandatory for a match are: LC card no. (010), ISBN (020). The presence or absence of a uniform title (130/240) does not matter when determining if a record is a match.

When in doubt as to an exact match, treat it as a match. If a record matches in edition, publisher, and pagination but has an earlier year or a different place of publication, treat it as a match. The number of intervening years between the date on the card and the date on the record is not important.

Marking the Card (Retrospective conversion through self-list card)

* When a match is found, write the OCLC number in the upper right hand corner of the shelflist card. If multiple matching records exist, choose the record with "DLC" in the 040 field. If a DLC record doesn't exist, then choose the record which has the most holdings.
* If you are unsure of a match existing, write the OCLC/ LOC number on the card with a "?" following. This number is located directly under the holdings information, i.e. OCLC: 234518, in the upper left hand area.
* If no match is found in OCLC, then write "0/OCLC" in the upper right hand corner of the shelflist card.

Create a new record

When a matching bibliographic record is not found in

OCLC, it is necessary to create one in OCLC. After the record is entered in OCLC and brought into database, the completion of the local holdings work outlined above remains to be done before conversion can be considered complete.

Records will be added to the database using the same standards as are followed for current copy cataloging.

Fields to be deleted

Fields to be deleted when transferring OCLC records into database

017, 018, 025, 033, 042, 046, 050, 055, 060, 069, 070, 071, 072, 080, 092, 096, 098, 210, 214, 222, 242, 263, 265, 302, 350, 510

Delete subject fields with indicators other than "0" (zero)

900 Delete these fields on monographic records

752, 753, 760-777 (on serials), 850, 852, 870-873, 886, 890

Delete all 9XX fields

* **GUIDELINES OF WHAT TO EDIT:**

i) Fix all typographical errors that occur in the 245 or any other indexed title field.

ii) If the 245, within the first five words, has a numeral or other words spelled out in [square brackets] or a symbol such as &, %, + add a 740 field spelling the word(s) out that appeared in square brackets or as a symbol. Delete any square brackets and the text within them from the 245. For instance, if the 245 in the online record appeared as: The story of the 2nd [i.e. second] day, you would add a 740 field reading: Story of the second day. and would change the 245 to read: The story of the 2nd day. If the 245 had a title of: The power & the glory, you would add a 740 field reading: Power and the glory. and would not edit the 245 at all.

iii) Fix all problems with filing indicators.

iv) Delete all initial articles occurring in 4xx, 6xx, 7xx, or 8xx | t fields.

v) If the date in the online record is different from the date on the cards (and the record is still considered a match):

  * You may edit the date in the fixed field and the 260 |c subfield **IF** the date was one that was questioned and the date in the online record would mislead the public via the OPAC index (which is drawn from the first of the fixed field dates)

  * You should NOT edit the date if the fixed field is correct according to the MARC format, just to make it index differently in the OPAC. For instance, according to the MARC format, a date appearing as [191-?] would properly have dates in the fixed field of 1910 and 1919.

  * You should **NOT** edit the date in the fixed field or the 260 |c if the online record is for an earlier printing and we are using it to provide access to one or more later printings.

vi) If the cards indicate an accompanying piece (such as a supplement) represented by either a **+ 1 supplement** or a dashed on — entry to the side or a 500 note saying: **Accompanied by:** look to make certain that the online record contains reference to the supplement. Dashed on entries generally require separate bibliographic records if the bib record doesn't mention a supplement, the information can often be added in either a **300** |**e** field or as a **500** note. Be sure to treat as a multi-volume set in the copy holdings and create a MHLD statement according to normal cataloguing guidelines. Consult your supervisor if you have questions.

vii) Correct **significant** errors in the 300 |a field (pagination). For instance, if the card says **347 p.**, but the online record says **374 p.**, make the correction. Or if the card says **2 v. in 1**, but the online record says **2 v.**, make the correction. If, however, the difference in paging is the result of a minor difference in how preliminary or illustrated pages were counted, do not make the change.

Also, if the 300 field is completely lacking in the online information, key in the information for that field as it appears on the shelf list card.

5.1.2 Copy cataloguing from LOC (Library of Congress) URL: http://catalog.loc.gov/

Library of congress online catalogues are available for download. This is a open source database can be searched by title, author, ISBN, etc.

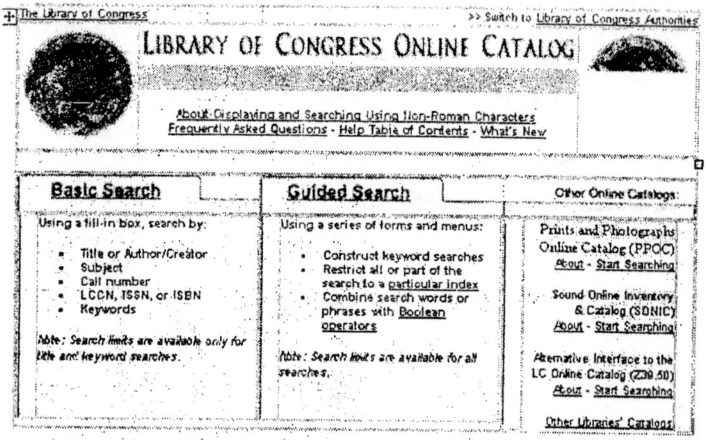

There are two option for searching the bibliographical record, basic search and guided search. Basic search is a simple search like a browse search. Guided search tips:

1. **Optional** : Set Search Limits before following the steps below.
2. **Search:** Enter a word, several words, or a phrase in the box.
3. From the following drop-down menu, select all of these, any of these or as a phrase ("all of these" is the default, and is highly recommended).
4. **As** : Select an Index Name* from the drop-down menu (Note: Number Searches are also available).
5. From the following radio buttons, select AND, OR, or NOT (boolean operators) to add more information to the

search (see Boolean Searching help page for assistance).

6. Repeat steps 2, 3 and 4 to refine your search further by using the last set of fill-in blanks and menus.

7. Select the 

to get results.

DATABASE: Library of Congress Online Catalog

5.2 Authority Control

Authority control is a critical component of the retrospective conversion process. It ensures that the headings (names, series, subjects, and uniform titles) on converted records are consistent with other heading in the catalogue and that those heading conform to current national standards. Optimal return on an investment in retrospective conversion requires a parallel investment in authority control.

OCLC/LOC input standards (whether for new or retrospective cataloguing) require that all name and series headings be established in AACR2 or AACR2 compatible form, if authority records are available. The standards require us to search the OCLC/LOC Authority File to verify forms of entry. Even if an authority record exists for the person in IO, OCLC/LOC input standards for original records require the cataloguer to check the national authority files immediately prior to creating a new record. Because authority records are sometimes revised (to take additional information into account), it is necessary to search OCLC/LOC for an authority record even if one for the person is found in IO. If those names are not in the authority file, OCLC/LOC encourages **but does not require** that the heading be constructed according to

AACR2 guidelines. We will use AACR2 forms when they are established and will apply the general rule of predominant form in most other cases.

Establishing the correct form of name for an author is a multi-step process. It involves looking at a number of factors and being aware of cataloguing conventions during different time periods to help interpret the information that you find. The following outlines some of the steps and points to consider.

Search the OCLC/LOC authority file for a matching authority record: Switch into the Authority File on OCLC/LOC.

* Perform a scan search for the personal name e.g.: sca pn waters, robert d

Be sure to include punctuation so that you will be placed into the correct spot in the scanned author index. Be sure to truncate the name somewhat (for instance, not include the complete middle name) to avoid missing a match that may vary slightly from the form on your book/card

/LOCIf a matching name authority record (rules "c" or "d") is found for the person (examine 400 notes, 670 notes, etc. to help decide), export the record into IO (<alt> <f12>)

Do not export the record into file if the identical authority record is already there.

Do not export the record into file if the "rules" are coded "a" or "b"

If no matching name authority record is found ("rules" "c" or "d"), mark the heading on the card as "0/AF" and proceed to the next step.

Establish the form of the name without an authority record.

* Search the OCLC/LOC bibliographic file for other occurrences of the author's name.

Perform an author search (4,3,1 = first four letters of the author's last name, first three letters of the author's first name, first letter of the middle name)

Examples:

Name on card:	Smith, Carol Ann, 1945-	search keys: smit,car,a
Name on card:	Ers, Fred	search keys: ers,fre,
Name on card:	Garcia Marquez, Gabriel	search keys: garc,gab,
Name on card:	El-Fadduz, Mohammed	search keys: elfa,moh,
Name on card:	McDonald, Roger P., 1909-	search keys: mdon,rog,p
Name on card:	Mcdonald, Robert Harold	search keys: mcdo,rob,h

Look for bibliographic records that seem to have the same author. Examine things such as publication dates, subjects, language of publication to help determine matches.

If there is a bibliographic record with the "desc" in the fixed field coded as "a" **AND** the 040 field is DLC | c DLC, use the form of the name as it appears in this bibliographic record, regardless of other forms that may appear in other records (if you are certain that it is the same author)

* If there are multiple bibliographic records with variations in the form of the author's name, determine the form of the name that the author used most frequently. Use the predominant form as the basis for the name heading

  a. Examine not only the 100 (or 700) field, but also examine statements of responsibility (| c of the 245 and sometimes 500 notes). Statements of responsibility reflect the way that the author's name appeared on the title page

In Pre-ISBD or ISBD records, the statement of responsibility was not transcribed if it exactly matched the heading for the name. Therefore, on a record catalogued according to pre-ISBD or ISBD rules where there is no statement of responsibility, you may assume that the form of the name in the heading matched the way it appeared on the publication

  b. If variations in form of the author's name are equally divided, prefer headings on the bibliographic records in the following order of preference of 040 fields:

DLC | c DLC (indicates the cataloguing was done by the Library of Congress and the machine record was created by the Library of Congress)

i. DLC | x XXX - [XXX stands for anything other than DLC] (indicates the cataloguing was done by the Library of Congress but the machine record was created by another library)

ii. XXX | c XXX (cataloguing done by a library other than the Library of Congress and the machine record was created by another library)

If there are not other bibliographic records to determine a predominant form of the author's name, use the form as it appears on the shelf list card.

Be alert to possible conflicts in name headings in the OCLC or IUCAT database. Add qualifiers as needed to distinguish the name you are establishing from another similar name in the database

Library of Congress On line Authority Heading Search: Using *Library of Congress Authorities*, you can browse and display authority headings for Subject, Name, Title and Name/Title combinations. You can also download authority records in MARC format for use in a local library system. This service is offered free of charge. Search tips:

http://authorities.loc.gov/

Search TypeBrief Help (select a search type for detailed Help)

General Tips
- All searches are "left-anchored" (enter search starting with leftmost word)
- Keyword searching is not available
- Omit all punctuation (including "—" in subject headings)
- Drop initial articles for titles
- Truncation is automatic

Subject
- Searches LC Subject Headings and

	Annotated Card Program (AC) Headings
	- Does not search free-floating subdivisions directly **Examples :** united states history civil war 1861 1865 regimental histories bible n t criticism interpretation etc persian gulf war 1991
Name	- Searches personal, corporate, meeting, and jurisdiction headings - For personal names, enter surname first - For group names, enter in direct order **Examples:** clemens samuel langhorne 1835 1910 twain mark 1835 1910 snodgrass quintus curtius 1835 1910 army war college u s russia federation
Title	- Searches uniform and series titles **Examples:** bible english new american standard king and i motion picture symphony #5 in e flat sibelius choreographic work guidi
Name/Title	- Searches headings combining author/ creator name and uniform title - Use Name Authority Headings search first to verify exact name heading *Examples:* shakespeare william 1564 1616 works 1997 poe edgar allan 1809 1849 short stories selections hugo victor 1802 1885 angelo tyran de padoue .

Example:

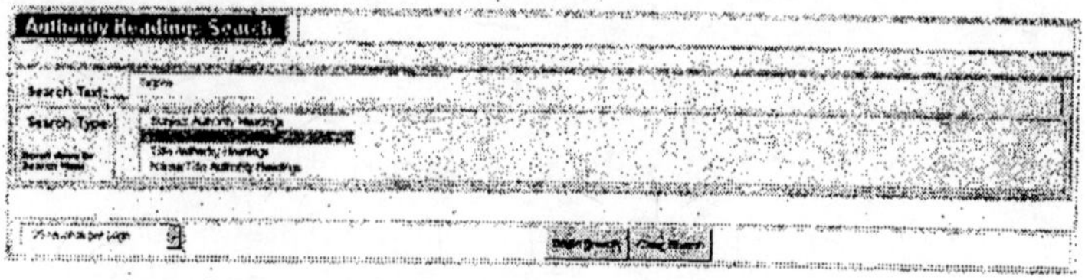

SOURCE OF HEADINGS: Library of Congress Online Catalog

YOU SEARCHED: Name Authority Headings = tagore

SEARCH RESULTS: Displaying 1 through 25 of 25.

◀ **Previous** **Next** ▶

	#	*Bib Records*	*select icon in first column to... View Authority Headings /References*	*Type of Heading*
	1	1	Tagore, Joteendro Mohun, maha ra ja baha dur, Sir, 1831-1908, [from old catalog]	personal name
References	2	0	Tagore, Jyotirindranath, 1849-1925	personal name
References	3	0	Tagore, Kadambari, 1859-1884	personal name
	4	2	Tagore law lectures, 1884. [from old catalog]	meeting name
	5	2	Tagore law lectures, 1897. [from old catalog]	meeting name
	6	1	Tagore law lectures, 1929. [from old catalog]	meeting name
	7	1	Tagore law lectures, 1935. [from old catalog]	meeting name
	8	1	Tagore law lectures, 1942. [from old catalog]	meeting name
Authorized Heading	9	0	Tagore, Lina	personal name

	#	*Bib Records*	*select icon in first column to... View Authority Headings /References*	*Type of Heading*
	10	1	Tagore Memorial Students' Library. Madurai, India. [from old catalog]	corporate name
References	11	0	Tagore, P. N., 1907-1965	personal name
	12	1	Tagore, Pramod Kumar. [from old catalog]	personal name
References	13	0	Tagore, Prosonocoomar, 1801-1868	personal name
	14	1	Tagore, Prossonno Coomar.	personal name
Authorized Heading	15	1	Tagore, Prossonno Coomar, 1801-1868.	personal name
	16	2	Tagore, Prossono Coomar, 1801-1868, [from old catalog]	personal name
Authorized Heading	17	0	Tagore, Protima	personal name
References	18	0	Tagore, Rabindra Nath, Sir, 1861-1941	personal name
Authorized Heading	19	892	Tagore, Rabindranath, 1861-1941	personal name
Authorized Heading	20	0	Tagore, Rabindranath, 1861-1941 (Spirit)	personal name
References	21	0	Tagore, Rabindranath Ghosh	personal name
References	22	0	Tagore, Rabindranath, Sir, 1861-1941	personal name
References	23	1	Tagore, Rathindranath, 1888-1961.	personal name
	24	1	Tagore, Rathindranath, 1888- [from old catalog]	personal name
Authorized Heading	25	5	Tagore Research Institute.	corporate name

MARC Display | Labelled Display

LC Control Number:	n 80036680
HEADING:	Tagore, Rabindranath, 1861-1941
000	03422cz a2200673n 450
001	3299002
005	20060120051939.0
008	800331n| acannaabn a aaa
010	__ |**a** n 80036680 |**z** no 00055441 |**z** no 97075143
035	__ |**a** (OCoLC)oca00418818
040	__ |**a** DLC |**b** eng |**c** DLC |**d** DLC |**d** CSmH |**d** DLC |**d** DLC-ON |**d** OCoLC |**d** DLC |**d** DLC-ON |**d** SG-SiILA
053	_0 |**a** PK1719 |**b** PK1727
100	1_ |**a** Tagore, Rabindranath, |**d** 1861-1941
400	1_ |**a** Tagor, Rabindranat, |**d** 1861-1941
400	1_ |**a** Taigeer, |**d** 1861-1941
400	1_ |**a** T?ha¯ku¯ru, Ravi¯ndrana¯tha, |**d** 1861-1941
400	0_ |**a** Rabindranath Tagore, |**d** 1861-1941
400	0_ |**a** Ravi¯ndrana¯tha T?ha¯kura, |**d** 1861-1941
400	1_ |**a** T?ha¯kura, Ravi¯ndrana¯tha, |**d** 1861-1941
400	1_ |**a** Tha´kur, Rabi´ndrana´th, |**d** 1861-1941
400	1_ |**a** T?a¯ghu¯r, Ra¯bindra¯na¯t, |**d** 1861-1941
400	1_ |**a** Ta¯ju¯r, Ra¯bindra¯na¯t, |**d** 1861-1941

400 1_ |**a** T?agol, |**d** 1861-1941

400 0_ |**a** Ravi¯ntirana¯ta Ta¯ku¯r, |**d** 1861-1941

400 1_ |**a** Ta¯ku¯r, Ravi¯ntirana¯ta, |**d** 1861-1941

400 1_ |**w** nnaa |**a** Tagore, Rabindranath, |**c** Sir, |**d** 1861-1941

400 0_ |**a** Rabi¯ndrana¯tha T?ha¯kura, |**d** 1861-1941

400 1_ |**a** T?ha¯kura, Rabi¯ndrana¯tha, |**d** 1861-1941

400 0_ |**a** Ravindranatha Tagora, |**d** 1861-1941

400 0_ |**a** T?ai-ko-e^rh, |**d** 1861-1941

400 1_ |**a** Tagora, Ravindranatha, |**d** 1861-1941

400 0_ |**a** Ravi¯ndrana¯tha T?ha¯ku¯ru, |**d** 1861-1941

400 1_ |**a** Tha´kur, R. |**q** (Rabindrana´th), |**d** 1861-1941

400 1_ |**a** Tagore, Rabindra Nath, |**c** Sir, |**d** 1861-1941

400 0_ |**a** N~i-dban?-mgon-po, |**d** 1861-1941

400 0_ |**a** Zhu, Zhendan, |**d** 1861-1941

400 0_ |**a** Chu, Chen-tan, |**d** 1861-1941

400 0_ |**a** Ra¯bindar Na¯th T?aigaur, |**d** 1861-1941

400 1_ |**a** T?aigaur, Ra¯bindar Na¯th, |**d** 1861-1941

400 0_ |**a** Ravi¯ntirana¯t Ta¯ku¯r, |**d** 1861-1941

400 1_ |**a** Ta¯ku¯r, Ravi¯ntirana¯t, |**d** 1861-1941

670 __ |**a** His Gitanjali ... 1913.

670 __ |**a** His Maka¯kavi Sar Ravi¯ntirana¯ta Ta¯ku¯r arul?iya Pan~ca viya¯san?kal?, 1982: |**b** t.p. (Sar Ravi¯ntirana¯ta Ta¯ku¯r)

670 __ |**a** His Gi¯ta¯n~jali, 1949: |**b** t.p. (Rabi¯ndrana¯tha T?ha¯kura)

670 __ |**a** Letter from Sahitya Akademi, 7/6/84 |**b** (Rabindranath Tagore renounced knighthood. The title "Sir" should not be used in heading)

670 __ |**a** Collier's ency. |**b** (Tagore, Sir Rabindranath, 1861-1941)

670 __ |**a** Ency. Brit. |**b** (Tagore, Rabindranath, 1861-1941)

670 __ |**a** Ency. Amer. |**b** (Tagore, Rabindranath, 1861-1941)

670 __ |**a** Citra¯n?gada¯ ; Bida¯ya abhis´a¯pa, 1990: |**b** t.p. (Ravi¯ndrana¯tha T?a¯gora)

670 __ |**a** U¯rvas´i, 1953: |**b** t.p. (Ravi¯ndrana¯tha T?ha¯ku¯ru)

670 __ |**a** Fiala, P. Lyricka´ symfonie, p1978: |**b** container (R. Tha´kura)

670 __ |**a** Mala´ c?esk. encykl. |**b** (Tha´kur (Tagore), Rabindrana´th; b. May 6, 1861; d. July 8, 1941)

670 __ |**a** Das Gupta, K.N. Caliph for a day, 1916: |**b** t.p. (Sir Rabindra Nath Tagore)

670 __ |**a** Sn~an n?ag mkhan po Jo-bo N~i-dban?-mgon-pos mdzad pa?i glu thar sbyar ma, 2000: |**b** t.p. (Jo-bo N~i-dban?-mgon-po)

670 __ |**a** Talks in China, 1999: |**b** t.p. (Zhu Zhendan) p. 8 (the Chinese characters on t.p. form the name given to the port by his Chinese friends)

670 __ |**a** Gi¯ta¯njali¯, 2001: |**b** t.p. (Ra¯bindar Na¯th T?aigaur)

670 __ |**a** Canniya¯ci allatu tavaci¯lar, 2004: |**b** t.p. (Ravi¯ntirana¯t Ta¯ku¯r)

952 __ |a RETRO

953 __ |**a** xx00 |**b** vn79

5.3 Formats and Standards

The MARC 21 format are standards for the representation and communication of bibliographic and related information in machine readable form. It is a harmonized CAN/MARC and USMARC format. MARC 21 format is a set of codes and content designations defined for encoding machine readable records. Formats are defined for five types of data: Bibliographic, Holding, Authority, Classification and Community.

Here we are giving the standard format of MARC 21, Monograph cataloguing common code.

Note: For details about the MARC 21 format, user can see the another book "MARC 21: Cataloguing Format for 21st century.

5.3.1 MARC 21 communication format

MONOGRAPH CATALOGUING COMMON CODE

MARC records are composed of fixed (same place, same length) and variable fields. Fixed fields are in a Leader, and in fields 006, 007,and 008. In bibliographic utilities and local systems these fixed fields are broken out into named fields for ease of entry. At first fixed fields seem abstruse. Soon the more common ones will become second nature.

Fixed Fields

Type (LDR/06)

a = language material (always for book)

g = audiovisual material (also coded in 008/33, e.g., 008/33 v = video tape)

Bib lvl (LDR/07):

i = integrating resource

m = monograph (always for book = monograph)

s = serial (see Serials Cataloguing Cheat Sheet)

Enc lvl (LDR/17):

0 = full record book in hand

1 = full record book not in hand

2 = less than full record

8 = CIP record (upgrade)

I = OCLC full record

K = OCLC less than full

Des cat form (LDR/18)

a = AACR/ISBD

Date entered on file(008/00-05)

yymmdd

Date type (008/06):

s = single date

r = reprint dates

c = continuation

d = dead serial

e = detailed date

m = multiple dates

n = unknown (try to use q and guess decade)

q = date in question, e.g. 194u

t = publication & copyright dates

Date one (008/07-10):

year of publication (s,t), reprinting (r), or beginning (m)

Date two (008/11-14):

year of ending (m), original printing (r), or copyright (t)

use 9999 if still being published

Country (008/15-17)

at = Australia

enk = England

fr = France

gw = Germany

it = Italy

ja = Japan

ii = India

States (U.S.):

alu aku azu aru cau cou ctu deu dcu flu gau
hiu idu ilu inu iau ksu kyu lau mau mdu meu
miu mnu mou msu mtu nbu ncu ndu nhu nju nmu
nvu nyu ohu oku oru pau riu scu sdu tnu txu
utu vau vtu wau wiu wvu wyu

xxu = United States, state unknown

Provinces (Canada):

abc bcc mbc nfc nkc nsc ntc nuc onc pic quc snc ykc

xxc = Canada, province unknown

Illus (008/18-21):

Up to four codes may be used for monographs.

a = illustrated

b = maps*

c = ports*

d = charts*

e = plans*

f = plates

g = music*

h = facsims*

i = coats of arms*

j = geneal tables*

k = forms*

m = soundrecording

o = photographs

p = illuminations

* use also in 300 field

Target Audience (008/22) :

a = Preschool

b = Primary

c = Pre-adolescent

d = Adolescent

e = Adult

f = Specialized

g = General

j = Juvenile

Form of item (008/23):

blank = can be read by naked eye

a = microfilm

b = microfiche

d = large print

Nature of Contents 008/24-27):

a = abstracts, summaries

b = bibliographies (with 504)

c = catalogs

d = dictionaries

e = encyclopedias

f = handbooks

i = indexes

g = legel

m = thesis

p = programmed texts

r = directories

s = statistics

Govt pub (008/28):

blank (#)= not govt. pub.

a = Autonomous or semi-autonomous component

c = Multilocal

i = international body (e.g. UNESCO)

f = federal

l = local (towns, counties)

s = state, province

Conference publication (008/29)

0 = Not a conference publication

1 = Conference publication

Festschrift (008/30)

0 = not Festschrift

1 = Festschrift

Index (008/31):

0 = no index

1 = index

Undefined (008/32)contains a blank (#) or fill character (|)

LitF (008/33)

0 = nonfiction

1 = fiction

c = comic strips

d = drama

e = essays

f = novels

h = humour

i = letters

j = short stories

m = mixed forms

p = poetry

s = speeches

u = unknown

Biography (008/34)

= No biographical material

a = Autobiography

b = Individual biography

c = Collective biography

d = Contains biographical information

| = No attempt to code

Lang (008/35-37):

language of text or predominate language

eng = English

fre = French

ger = German

spa = Spanish

Modified record (008/38)

Cataloguing Source (008/39):

source of cataloging

blank = DLC

d = local library

Variable Fields

010 LC card order number; not usually on a typed card;lower right corner of an LC printed card. Key in MARC record with three blank spaces as front, and 0's in needed replacing "-" to equal 8 spaces.

020 International Standard Bibliographic Number (ISBN); if given on card, usually last note (see 500). In MARC record, key without hyphens.

024 With first indicator 3, International Artical Number (EAN); may replace or be in addition to 020 ISBN for some monographs; ISBNs become EANs by having 978 refixed, and the check digit recalculated.

041 Language codes for translations and multilingual items, since 008/35-47 will only contain one language code.

043 Geographic code used whenever there's a 651 or 650 | z

050 Library of Congress call number (LCC); not given on typed card; to left of hole of an LC printed card. In MARC record key as 050 2nd indicator 0 (assigned at LC) or 4 (local), e.g.:

050 4 $aAB1234.5$b.D78 1998, or if two Cutters, 050 4

$aAB123.5.C6$bD78 1999. Note period for first Cutter, $b for second, both for one Cutter, but only one of each.

082 Dewey Decimal call number (DDC); not given on typed card; next to LC call number on LC printed card. 2nd indicator 0 if assigned by LC, 4 if local. Omit Cutter. Use " / " to indicate natural breaks. On OCLC locally assigned DDC numbers plus Cutter are keyed in 092.

090 Local call number; MARC tag number varies with system. e.g.:

090 0 $aAB/1234.5/C6/D78/1998$bMAIN$c1-2$d1-2 ($b = location, $ccopies, $dvolumes) On OCLC keyed like 050 and used for locally assigned LCC numbers. Usually one of the above numbers, is in the upper left hand corner of the card. A new line is normally begun with each Cutter.

092 See 082.

100 Author; if the work has three or fewer authors (and that is authors, not compilers or editors) the first is given, surname first, at first indentation, opposite the 2nd line of the call number (usually 2 spaces). A compiler *is* the author of an index or bibliography however. In MARC records key 1st indicator 1 for surname, e.g.: 100 1 $aSmith, Jones,$d1932- [This and all 1XX and 7XX fields are normally checked against the library's or LC's authority file to achieve uniformity.]

110 If the work is the annual report of a corporate body, the report of a task force, or some such, the corporate body

is the author. There are fewer corporate bodies as author (main entry) under current rules than earlier. On cards the corporate author begins 2 spaces after the second line of the call number, and wraps to 2 spaces in from that. In MARC records, key 1st indicator 1 for a corporate body which begins with a jurisdiction, 2 for direct order, e.g.: 110 1 $aCanada.$bDept. of State. 110 2 $aCanadian Unitarian Council.

111 If what you have is conference proceedings, the name of the conference is the author. In a MARC record the name is followed by $n(number :$ddate :$cPlace), or if no number, $d(date :$cPlace).

BUT 110$aCorporate Name.$bConference$n(... The subfield codes, e.g. "$n" above, shown in these examples are a single space on cards.

On cards, placement is the same as corporate author.

130 Uniform title as main entry. If the work is an anonymous classic such as the Bible, Arabian Nights, or Chicken Little, that common title (known as a uniform title) goes in 130 or in author position on the book/card. For the Bible you give language and date. For parts of the Bible you start with Bible, e.g., in a MARC record; 130 $aBible.$pO.T.$pGenesis$lEnglish$f1995 On cards, placement is same as corporate author.

240 Uniform title as filing title; only after a 100 or 110. (Both 130 and 240 being called uniform title shows how MARC works as a check list better than words.) For classical music, laws, and very voluminous authors like Shakespeare, most libraries have a title which brings the same works together. To construct one, best look at some in the catalogue for examples (as with 130s). The uniform title goes on the card under the author, usually 4 spaces in from where the author began. It is in square brackets, and wraps to 2 spaces in. Do not use square brackets for the MARC record.

245 The title as on the title page; use a ":" before subtitles,

(:$b in MARC) "=" before a title in another language; followed by "/" and up to three authors. If more than three, give the first followed by "... [et al.]." (The title is the main entry in this case, i.e., no 100.) If they did different things, use a ";", e.g. /$cby John Smith ; illustrated by Tim Jones. Only the first word and proper names are capitalized. Names of Acts are proper names. All German nouns are capitalized. On a card, the title begins under the author, 4 spaces in, and wraps to 2 spaces in. (That is 4 and 2 spaces from where the author began, not from the edge of the card.)

Each field within this (and any) paragraph is separated from the following by a " — " on cards. The "—" is not keyed in MARC records because it is system supplied where used. If there is no author or 130 (i.e. title main entry), the title begins at first indentation (where the author would have begun) and wraps to 2 spaces in. This is called "hanging indentation". In a MARC record, use 1st indicator 0 for title main entry, 1 (for title added entry) if there is a 1XX, 2nd indicator for number of spaces to be skipped in filing, e.g., A = 2, An = 3, and The - 4, because of the space following the initial article, e.g.: 245 14 $aThe story of my life :$ban autobiography /$cby Tom Jones.

245$h[gmd] If the item is nonbook, a general material designation follows the first title proper. It is enclosed in square brackets in both MARC records and on cards. (Some old OCLC records will be found without the brackets.) Common ones are:

cartographic material

electronic resource

kit

microform

sound recording

videorecording

When there is a gmd, there is also an smd, a more specific term in 300. For example, a sound recording might be a sound disc or a sound cassette. See examples in AACR2 2002. Consult the index under the name of the form.

246 Alternate title which represents the whole work, e.g.:

246 31 $aParallel title

246 14 $aCover title

246 15 $aAdded title page title

246 1 $iAt head of title:$aPhrase at head of title 1st indicator 3 means added entry, no note; 1st indicator 1 means added entry and note; the second indicator says which print constant to use for the note; if no print constant is available, use ia as shown. For cards see 740.

247 Former title for a loose-leaf service or website (integrating entity) which changes title. I the future these may not be considered monographs.

250 Edition, e.g., 2nd ed. —, Rev. ed. — If a person wrote the edition, you would say so, e.g., Smith's chemistry. — 2nd ed.

/$bby Tim Jones. — On a card, the edition continues the paragraph begun by the title.

260 Imprint, e.g.:

260 $aNew York :$bSmith & Jones,$c1995.

On cards, the imprint ends the title paragraph, coming after the title or edition, with a " — " between.

300 Collation, e.g.:

300 $ax, 100 p. :$bill. ;$c23 cm.

If multiple volumes, the number of volumes is given, e.g., 3 v.

:$bill. ;$c28 cm. If the volumes are numbered right through (as opposed to each volume starting with page 1, then, 3 v. (300 p.)

:$bgraphs ;c26 cm. Other possible variations include 1

v. (various pagings)* ;$c28 cm., 1 v (unpaged) ; 28 cm., (Loose-leaf is used for material to be updated, not just anything in a binder.) On a card, the collation starts a new paragraph 4 spaces in, and wraps to 2 spaces in. For nonbook material smd, see 245$h.

440 Series. If it has a number or year, that goes after ;$v.

On cards in the same paragraph as the collation, in parenthesis, separated by " — ".

490 Series differing from the way it is entered in the catalogue.

1st indicator 1 in the MARC record means traced form is in 830 Don't use 490 0, untraced series; instead quote in 500, e.g.,

"Penguin books." A series with a subject word would be 440 or 490 1, without in a quoted 500.

500 General notes. There are also specific notes. As a beginner, if you see something which seems helpful on the title page, just quote it, e.g., 500 $a"Reports the law as of April 1, 1995." Notes go below the collation/series paragraph, usually skipping a space, each note beginning a new paragraph 4 spaces in, wrapping to 2.

Some other common notes include:

502 Thesis, e.g., Thesis (PhD)—Podunk University, 1995.

504 Includes bibliographic references and index.

505 Contents, e.g., v. 1. Title one — v. 2. Title two.

525 How updated.

546 Language, e.g., Text in English and French on inverted pages.

Subjects. In MARC records, subject subdivisions have subfield codes

$xTopic$zPlace$yPeriod$vGenre.

600 Person as subject, in same format as person as author.

On cards, subjects (6XX) and added entries (7XX) all form one paragraph starting 4 spaces in, wrapping to 2, with no "—" between them. Subjects are numbered 1. 2., etc. Added entries are numbered I. II., etc. Usually a line is skipped between the last note and the first tracing, if it can be done without forcing you onto a second card. If you must do a second card, you say "(Continued on next card)" at the lower right of the card, start the next card with the author (or title if no author), the title (without subtitle) in the same paragraph (like a hanging indentation), "...", the date from 260$c, and "(Card 2)". Then continue with the information where you left off.

610 Corporate body as subject (including governments).

611 Conference as subject.

630 Uniform title as subject.

650 Topic as subject, e.g.:

650 0 $aChemistry$vPeriodicals.

650 0 $aChemsitry$xPeriodicals$v$vBibliography.

651 Place as subject (but not governments), e.g.:

651 0 $aCanada$xHistory$y1755-1763.

700 Person as added entry, e.g., the 2nd and 3rd of three authors, the first of more than three, editors.

710 Corporate body as added entry.

711 Conference as added entry.

740 Title added entries. (Now in MARC titles which represent the whole work are coded 246, while titles which represent part of the work or a related work, are here.) On cards all title tracings are here. They are given as, for example: I. Title. [traces 245 where there is a 1XX] II. Title: Introduction to history. [traces a title different from 245, e.g, a distinctive subtitle]

830 Series entered in catalogue differently than on item. Series as on tem is in 490 1st indicator 1, and series as entered in the catalogue is here. On cards, series as on item is traced, e.g.,

III. Series. IV. Series: History for beginners. traces a

series in a form different from 490; this is done by most libraries when there is a slight variation in the way a publisher prints the series]

If you can still get at an old card catalogue, look at some cards. You will see older cards and NARC records done under earlier rules. Looking through a volume of the National Union Catalog would help as well.

Sample card:

900

S45h Smith, John, 1950-

History for beginners : introduction to history / by John Smith and Tim Jones. — 2nd. ed. — New York : Smith & Jones, 1995.

x, 100 p. :$bill. ; 23 cm. — History textbooks ; no 5.

Includes bibliographical references and index.

1. History. I. Jones, Tim. II. Title. II. Title: Introduction.to history. III. Series.

5.3.2 Standard for cataloguing

Different types of Cataloguing rules are available i.e. CCC (Classified Cataloguing Code), ISBD (International Standard Bibliography Description) and AACR-II (Anglo American Cataloguing Rules-II). But most popular and used to standards tool for cataloguing is AACR-II 1998. The 2002 revision of the AACR, included the major overhaul of the rules dealing.

5.3.3 Standard for subject heading

For subject heading, Library of Congress Subject Heading are being used.

LCSH reasonably simple, straightforward and efficient for organizations where cost and personnel limitations are common place. It is a vocabulary that provides a common thread or a set of controlled access points across the disciplines. It is useful for both general and high-level subject description. It provides an often broadly focused, controlled vocabularly to supply useful subject terms. LCSH is a standardized descriptive language familiar to librarians in all disciplines.

5.3.4 Standard for classification

A **library classification** is a *system* of coding and organizing library materials (*books*, serials, audiovisual materials, computer files, *maps, manuscripts*, realia) according to their subject. A classification consists of tables of subject headings and *classification* schedules used to assign a class number to each item being classified, based on that item's subject.

Until the *19th century*, most libraries had closed stacks, so the library classification only served to organize the subject *catalog*. In the *20th century*, libraries opened their stacks to the public and started to shelve the library material itself according to some library classification to simplify subject browsing.

There are many standard systems of library classification in use, and many more have been proposed over the years. These include the *Library of Congress classification* (LC) and the *Dewey Decimal Classification* (DDC), which are the most common systems in the *English*-speaking world. Other less commonly used classification systems include the *Bliss bibliographic classification*, the *Colon classification* and the *Universal Decimal Classification*. These systems are often considered to be theoretically superior, since they make use of the principle of synthesis (combining codes from different lists to represent the different attributes of a work), which is comparatively lacking in LC or DDC.

There are three main types of classification systems:

* *enumerative* - produce an alphabetical list of subject

headings, assign numbers to each heading in alphabetical order

* *hierarchial* - divides subjects hierarchially, from most general to most specific
* *faceted or analytico-synthetic* - divides subjects into mutually exclusive orthogonal facets

The most common classification systems, LC and DDC, are essentially enumerative, though with some hierarchial and faceted elements, especially at the broadest and most general level. The first true faceted system was the *Colon classification* of *S. R. Ranganathan.*

Specialist classification systems have been developed for particular subject areas, and some specialist libraries develop their own classification system that emphasises those areas they specialise in. An example specialist classification system for *art* and iconography is *Iconclass.*

Library classification forms part of the field of *library and information science.*

5.5 Useful tools for Retrospective Conversion

5.5.1 Book where - for windows

BookWhere [WebClarity]

http://www.webclarity.info/

products/bookwhere.html

The BookWhere Client for Windows allows you to search thousands of library catalogues and related databases including academic, public, and national libraries worldwide. BookWhere, equipped with a current AutoSync subscription, is capable of searching any of these *databases.*

Features:

* Powerful, simultaneous (spray) searching
* Immediate results display
* Ease of use
* Customize for your bibliographic searching style

* **AutoSync** *feature keeps your list of Z39.50* **databases** *up to date with WebClarity Software, Inc.'s* **Resource Registry**
* Multilingual user interface (English, French, Spanish, German, and Italian)
* Supports international database searching
* *Fully* **Bath** *Level 0 and 1 compliant*
* Supports MARC, UNIMARC, UKMARC, DanMARC, MAB1, SUTRS and GRS-1 Record Types
* MARC Notepad editing tool integration available
* Export records in MARC, TEXT, XML, Ibidem, Citation 7/8, Inmagic, Procite and Reference Manager formats

5.5.2 Dewey for windows

Dewey Decimal (DDC)

Products

http://

www.oclc.org/dewey/

versions/default.htm

Dewey for Windows (DFW) is a windows-based product designed for use with a CD-ROM that contains the Dewey Decimal Classification system. Dewey for Windows lets you point and click your way through DDC functions and includes

Windows format that allows you to drag and drop information between windows

* Expanded search and display options
* An ability to display multiple DDC records from the schedules, tables, index, and Manual on one screen
* An ability to share a single CD-ROM drive among multiple users on a LAN
* An extensive Help system that includes the Glossary and Introduction from the print DDC

Dewey for Windows Guide that gives detailed instructions on records, searching. and number building;

provides additional assistance in mastering Dewey for Windows for classification.

At the broadest level, the DDC is divided into ten main classes, which together cover the entire world of knowledge. These classes are further divided into ten divisions and each division into ten sections, although not all the numbers for the divisions and sections have been used. (The word class may be used to indicate main classes, divisions, sections, and any other notational level in the hierarchy.)

The ten main classes are:

000	Generalities
100	Philosophy & psychology
200	Religion
300	Social sciences
400	Language
500	Natural sciences & mathematics
600	Technology (Applied sciences)
700	The arts Fine and decorative arts
800	Literature & rhetoric
900	Geography & history

Main class 000 is the most general class, and is used for works not limited to any one specific discipline, e.g., encyclopedias, newspapers, general periodicals. This class is also used for certain specialized disciplines that deal with knowledge and information, e.g., computer science, library and information science, journalism. Main classes 100 - 900 each consist of a major discipline or group of related disciplines.

5.5.3 The OCLC Four-Figure Cutter Tables

The OCLC Four-Figure Cutter Tables are revised and expanded versions of the Cutter Three-Figure Author Table and the Cutter-Sanborn Three-Figure Author Table. The expansion balanced the distribution of main entries over the Cutter table entries. The expanded OCLC Four-Figure Cutter Tables are compatible with the existing two-figure or three-figure schemes.

Download the file cutter.exe to your computer's hard disk: On the OCLC web site, go to

< http://www.oclc.org/dewey/products/index.htm#cutter>

Under Dewey Cutter Software, click Download now.

The OCLC Four-Figure Cutter Tables are revised and expanded versions of:

* Cutter Three-Figure Author Table
* Cutter-Sanborn Three-Figure Author Table

The expansion balances the distribution of main entries over the Cutter table entries. The expanded OCLC Four-Figure Cutter Tables are compatible with the existing two-figure or three-figure schemes.

Before beginning to use the Dewey Cutter Program, decide which cutter scheme you need. The software can generate cutter numbers according to both the Cutter Four-Figure Table and the Cutter-Sanborn Four-Figure Table.

5.5.4 MarcEdit

MarcEdit 4.6 is the latest and greatest version of MarcEdit. New additions were made to the script maker (you can now edit scripts that your created with the script maker), the delimited text translator (more robust) the global editing tools (particularly the Swap field function), the Z39.50 Client and the XSLT crosswalks distributed with the program.

The MarcEditor module takes the place of the Edit window found in the previous version of MarcEdit. In the previous version, the edit window allowed the user to edit and create MARC records inside of the application. The MarcEditor takes this function a step further, embedding a fully functioning wordpad into the MarcEdit application. The MarcEditor is still linked to the MarcMaker for quick MARC file creation, in addition to adding a number of new features aimed at making record creation a little bit simpler. For example, the MarcEditor includes a field counter, a search and replace function, a Global Delete and Add Field option, as well as a spell checker for checking words and phrases.

Wizards:

The application contains two wizard to help users customize their version of MarcEdit. These wizards are the 1) Diacritics Wizard and 2) the Plugin Wizard. The Diacritics wizard allows users to specify custom diacritics to be used, in addition to the default diacritics support. The second wizard, the Plugin Wizard, allows users to create their own solutions, and integrate them into the MarcEdit application.

MARC Edit Tools

* MARC Tools Main Window: Access the main MARC Tools Dialog to access all the MARC conversions currently registered with the application.
* MARC Breaker: The MARC Breaker allows users to break MARC data into a plain, mnemonic text file.
* MARC Maker: The MARC Maker allows users to compile MARC Edit's mnemonic format back into MARC.
* MARC=>MARCXML: The MARC=>MARCXML conversion is the cornerstone of Marc Edit's XML API schema, providing a base conversion layer for all other conversion types (EAD, MODS, Dublin Core, etc.)
* MARC Editor: The MARC Editor is Marc edit's built-in notepad designed for editing MARC records.
* MARC Edit Z39.50 Client: The MarcEdit Z39.50 Client is a freeware add-on to the MarcEdit application. The MarcEdit Z39.50 Client provides MarcEdit users with a native Z39.50 client integrated into the MarcEdit Suite.
* MARC Edit Script Maker: The MarcEdit Script Maker can openned via the MarcEdit main menu's Add-in function, or by selecting MarcEdit Script Maker from the Start/Programs/MarcEdit directory or the Main MarcEdit Screen.

PART III : INTEGRATED LIBRARY SYSTEMS

Chapter 6
Acquisition System

6.1 Acquisition System

This system covers the acquisition process of library material including books, government documents, CD-ROM, electronic resources. Generally it referred to ordering the books, receiving and payment.

6.2 Functions of Automated Acquisition System

The Acquisition system functions as the central order and payment area for library materials including books, serials and periodicals, non-print items, electronic journals and databases, CD's and videos. We do this by investigating the fastest method of acquiring the items at the best cost. In other words, we try to get what you need at a good price and as quickly as possible. We are committed to the needs and concerns of the staff, faculty, researchers and all library users.

The library acquisitions department strives to acquire materials in all formats for the library collection quickly, efficiently and economically along with effectively spending the materials budget in a timely manner.

6.2.1 Selection of library materials

Academic staff and the committee carry out selection predominantly – library suggestions are accepted from faculty, students, and general staff. The acquisitions team with the end of the previous semester obtains recommended texts.

The librarian, library committee, and the faculty members are authorized to select the library materials. The library acquires that materials through book fairs, lists provided by library vendors, lists provided in publishers, catalogues, and the physical presence of books on direct request of a Librarian, library committee, faculty member, or researcher.

6.2.2 Book order procedure

* The Acquisitions department receives orders either from the Librarian, faculty member or the Library committee.
* Requests can be submitted on the "**Book Requisition Form**", which is available at both campuses libraries' in paper form.
* The book requisition form can be submitted between 10:00 A.M. - 12:00 P.M. (daily) to the acquisition department at the main campus library. No order will be entertained after this time.
* Incomplete requests will not be entertained.
* Orders submitted by faculty members must have an authorized signature of the faculty member and the Head of Department as well.
* If a request has more than 2 copies of the same book then multiple copies will only be purchased when a title is recommended as a textbook (prescribed text) or a reference (recommended text) for a course offered.
* Items normally must be ordered significantly (2-3 months) before they are needed.
* The turnaround time will be 3-4 weeks, if item(s) is locally available.
* The turnaround time will be 8-10 weeks, if item(s) is not locally available.
* The requestor should also be notified, as soon as possible, if an item is not available for any reason, either out-of-print, not yet published, out of stock indefinitely, or if there is a great price discrepancy.
* We will place an order to the local vendor, supplier or directly to the publisher.

6.2.3 Rush orders

We process an order as a Rush Order if it is needed for immediate use. Keep in mind that Rush orders are ordered direct from a publisher, and so we do not benefit from the discounted prices that vendors offer. In addition, a Rush order is subject to extra handling and shipping costs per book. This is charged against the department ordering the item.

The turnaround time is 6-8 weeks for rush orders; if items of rush orders are locally available the turnaround time will be 2 weeks.

Creating Purchase Orders from Selection Lists: Staff with permission to create purchase orders may select items from the Title Selection List window and create a purchase order.

6.2.4 Non-print items

Audio Cassettes, Videos, and CD's, can be ordered by faculty and staff members. These orders are processed on the same requisition form.

6.2.5 Journals order orocedure

Journals are ordered by the Acquisitions Department. The Acquisitions Department produces departmental lists of journal titles that are purchased in support of each subject, since journals are purchased on a subscription basis for an academic calendar year.

Requests for new journals are considered throughout the year however; it is recommended that new requests be submitted no later than September prior to the calendar year in which the subscription is to start. This allows the vendor to place the order with the publisher in time for January. A new journal request is forwarded to the Chairperson, Library Committee and Director, where a variety of issues including shelving space, funds, and collection development are considered.

6.3 Integrated Library System for Acquisitions

The Acquisitions module must be fully integrated with all system modules and must support an unlimited number of material types/formats, funds, vendors, orders, claims and transactions, without added cost. The system must be dynamically updated in real time to maintain the currency of all records and statistics.

The Acquisitions module must support the following functions:

6.3.1 Fund management

The Acquisitions module must permit:

a. Temporary freezing of funds with override capability.

b. Freezing new order but permitting payment on outstanding orders.

c. Freezing both new orders and further payment.

The Acquisitions module must:

a. Enable each fund to be subdivided (categorized) by up to five levels.

b. Enable each subdivision to be used to group accounts together as an online workstation query.

c. Enable each subdivision to be used to group accounts together to report on spending in the different categories.

d. Allow remaining allocations to be carried over from one fiscal year to the next, if desired.

The Acquisitions module must enable an authorized operator to:

a. Create new accounts at any time.

b. Enter an initial allocation when an account is first created.

c. Update an account at any time.

d. Close out an account at any time, so long as there are no outstanding encumbrances against it.

For each fund, the Acquisitions module must maintain the following information, which must be available through online display, without the need to generate a report:

a. The original budget allocation.

b. Dollar amount of orders outstanding (encumbered).

c. Dollar amount of orders paid, the free balance.

d. Cash balance, the number of items on order.

e. Number received.

f. Number paid for.

g. Number of orders placed for the fund.

The Acquisitions module must allow multiple distribution methods, including:

a. Library-defined holdings code.

b. Directly to requestor's address.

c. Indirectly to requestor with shipment to library for processing.

6.3.2 Vendor records

The Acquisitions module must support an unlimited number of vendor records, accessible by vendor name (complete), vendor name (truncated), and vendor number. The vendor record must include at least order and remittance addresses, library-supplied vendor claim period indicator, and performance statistics.

The vendor file must include performance statistics updated automatically and in real time, available online and through reports, that include, but are not limited to:

a. Average receipt period in days.

b. Number of claims sent.

c. Number of copies cancelled.

d. Number of copies claimed.

e. Total amount ordered.

f. Amount encumbered.

g. Amount invoiced.

h. Amount paid.

i. Total number of orders.

j. Number of copies not received.

k. Number of copies paid.

l. Average order price.

m. Average price paid.

n. Average discount.

o. Supply times

Vendor records must support up to three distinct addresses per vendor, such as ordering, service, and marketing, and also provide notes / comment fields for Library staff.

6.3.3 Add purchase order

The Acquisitions module must support an unlimited number of order records. Order records must be searchable by bibliographic information, including item ID. Orders must be searched, browsed, or exactly matched by order ID, author, call number, general, medical subject, periodical title, series, subject, title and title control number. Packing list and requisition numbers must also be searchable. Order line searching must also supported. Acquisitions staff must be able to specify the fiscal cycle and acquisitions to search.

The Acquisitions module must prevent duplicate order ID numbers. An alert must be provided staff before the order is saved to the database.

The Acquisitions module must:

a. Prevent assignment of duplicate order numbers, whether entered manually or assigned automatically.

b. Support electronic submission of orders.

c. Support electronic data interchange (EDI).

d. Accommodating multi-institutional and multi-fund shared acquisitions.

e. Link order records to the corresponding bibliographic record.

f. Report the current status of any and all titles ordered or received.

g. Use status information to signal for a variety of activities, such as produce purchase order, delete order, produce open order report, etc.

h. Enable an authorized operator to access orders through the catalog, vendor, account, and requester.

6.3.4 Creating purchase order from selection records

The Acquisitions module must support selection lists with access controlled by user login and password.

The Acquisitions module must:

a. Provide a selection list feature whereby titles the Library intends to order may be kept online.

b. Accommodate desiderata files, that may also generate "consider for re-activation" reports based on dates incorporated from the desiderata records.

c. Allow staff to vote on purchase decisions.

d. Must automatically link purchase requests to items contained in a selection file, which can be hidden from public view and made accessible only to authorized users.

6.3.5 Receipt of materials

The Acquisitions module must automatically determine how to handle a partial receipt of ordered items, based upon Library policies. Describe.

A receipt records the arrival of ordered material and is attached to a purchase order. It follows that before you can receive line items, a purchase order must exit. Further, you cannot enter receipt information for a purchase order unless that order has the status ordered, which means that the order has been transmitted. All receipt activity takes place on the receipts window.

The receipts function lets you add, update, view, and delete receipts that are directly related to ONE purchase order. In the case of a Serial order, the function lets you add, update, view, and delete the first expected issue.

For every purchase order line item, you can choose a receipt status from a full-down list box in the Edit Receipt Information. Software provides a number of preset receipt statuses, but your library will want to define its own.

Not received, received satisfactorily, Receive not satisfactorily, Referred to a supervisor, hold pending investigation, Returned.

Assigning a condition to indicate a special type, status, or condition of receipt. Your library can define condition values in the acquisitions parameters. Some samples of conditions: correct, damaged item, defective item, duplicate, wrong title, wrong edition.

Adding to the new book list: If you select On New Book List check box on the Edit receipt information dialog box, the item in the database so that it will be included in a New Book List report. Print the receipt slip. Your library can customize the receipt slip by editing or translating the default file.

6.3.6 Invoice management

The Acquisitions module must support an unlimited number of invoice records. Staff must have the option to search and retrieve invoices by: invoice ID and optionally, a line number, a vendor ID, or a check number. Staff must be able to specify whether to display summary information, extended information, amounts, dates, and/or numbers associated with invoices.

The invoicing function lets you record invoices as they are received from a vendor and link them to the associated purchase orders. It consists adding, updating, viewing, and deleting invoices and invoice line items.

Currency rule

The currency chosen at the time of invoice may be different from the currency used for the purchase order. The currency chosen for the invoice must be the same as for the voucher payment Fluctuations in currency exchange rate values are not dynamically updated. Libraries are responsible for updating currency exchange rates in accordance to their established policies.

Add Invoice number in the purchase order, software verifies that this is valid invoice for the vendor you selected during ordering and generate a invoice is created for payment.

6.3.7 Voucher

The voucher function is used to pay invoices. A voucher may be used to pay multiple invoices provided they are from the same vendor. In addition, vouchers may be paid in whole or in part.

6.3.8 Payment

Add invoice window displays the home currency by default, but if you want, you can choose another currency for the invoice. About the invoice taxes, the software will automatically calculate the tax on an invoice or invoice line item based on the percent specified in the parameter and will automatically charge the tax, whether it is applied to the invoice or an invoice line item, to the specified accounts.

Payment vouchers with invoice: Create a new payment voucher or view an existing one that contains a list of invoice eligible for payment and belonging to a specified vendor.

Credit: Generally two types of credits, specific and internal, which you can assign when you create a credit record. Specific credit: This credit is linked directly to a vendor and used against any future invoice presented for payment. Internal credit: This credit is created internally and used to adjust the expenditure for an account, for example, when an order for partially paid item is cancelled.

6.3.9 Reminder claiming /cancellation of orders

The Acquisitions module must be able to automatically generate a claim/cancellation letter to the appropriate vendor regarding copies/volumes canceled and the reason. The

Acquisitions module must be able to transmit claims and cancellations via letter, email, or X12.

If an order passes its library-defined 'date to claim', the system must automatically add a claim segment to the appropriate outstanding line items on the order. Each claim segment must include a claim reason, number of copies claimed, times claimed, part or volume claimed (for multi-part items), date mailed, vendor response, date of vendor response, and claim status (OPEN, RECEIVED, CANCELLED.) The system must update elements in the claim segment automatically.

6.3.10 Gift items

When gifts or legal deposits are received, Virtua provides a way to both record and acknowledge receipt via the 541 tag of the MARC bibliographic record. The information from the sub fields in the 541 tag are used to generate acknowledgment letters.

Complete the record, using all required fields as well as the541 tag (Immediate Source of Acquisition), which contain additional information needed for the acknowledgment letter.

$a - Source of acquisition (NR) The name of the person or organization that is the of the material.

$b - Address (NR)

$c - Method of acquisition (NR) The terms under which a transfer of physical custody occurs for example, by gift, loan, or purchase.

$d - Date of acquisition (NR)

$e - Accession number (NR) The identification code assigned to materials acquired in a single and separate transfer of custody.

$f - Owner (NR) The individual or organization with legal custody over the described materials.

$h - Purchase price (NR)

$n - Extent (R) The number of items acquired.

$o - Type of unit (R) The name of the unit of measurement, for example, cartons.

Chapter 7
Cataloguing System

7.1 Cataloging Records in the MARC Editor

This system covers the concepts of cataloging and authority control. The Bibliographic Control/Cataloging module must allow the Library to create and maintain full catalog records searchable only by library staff.

The Bibliographic Control/Cataloging module must provide Cataloging wizards that streamline the process of:

* Adding a brief title record
* Editing existing titles
* Duplicating an existing title
* Removing title, call number/volume or copies
* Creating and editing call number/volume records
* Adding or editing copies (includes global edits)
* Offering authority control options (display, add, duplicate, edit, remove)
* Bound-with processing is straightforward
* Providing access to a cataloging review file
* Transferring title, call number or copies
* Linking order line holdings to titles
* Capturing and editing records from Z39.50 sources using a Z39.50 copy cataloging client

When duplicating a title, authorized staff must be able to pre-set values within the Cataloging wizard, including but not limited to:

* The automatic addition of a 006 field
* Hiding the record display from the Web OPAC (from public user searches)

* Item type (to prevent repetitive data entry)
* Item price
* Statistical categories
* Record format (e.g., MARC, Dublin Core, Map, etc.)
* Auto-generate temporary call numbers
* Whether to add a copy automatically when adding a call number/volume record
* Whether to auto-generate an item ID when adding a copy/item
* Ability to validate authority headings (if authority control is used by Library)
* Printing spine labels

When removing a title, call number, and/or item record, the Bibliographic Control/Cataloging module must alert staff if a bill or hold is associated with the material. Staff must be able to immediately investigate the open transaction, without closing the removal process.

When using the Bound-with process to link bibliographic descriptions for items bound together, the Bibliographic Control/Cataloging module must use parent and child call number records. A child call number with copies must not be bound with a parent call number. A child call number must be linked to only one parent, but staff must be able to link a parent call number to an **unlimited** number of child call numbers.

In the transferring title, call number/volume, and/or copies process, authorized staff must be able to:

* Transfer all copies to an existing call number
* Transfer only selected copies
* Transfer all volumes
* Transfer only selected volumes
* Remove a title automatically after staff elect to transfer the last copy or volume to a new title

* Search and display bibliographic information without exiting the transfer process

Items on reserve or in transit must not be transferred. Inactive, available title-level holds linked to a call number must also block the transfer. The Bibliographic Control/Cataloging module must alert staff to such exception conditions when staff attempt to transfer records.

At Library staff's discretion, records may be hidden from public user display at the title level (to hide bibliographic data and all associated items), the call number level (to hide selected volumes and all associated copies), item level (to hide selected copies), or by assigning the item to a "shadowed" location.

The Bibliographic Control/Cataloging module must support MARC format error checking, including:

* Error checking (tags, indicators, and sub fields) for all formats
* An error message displays when incorrect values are entered
* Prompts for correct data
* Automatically verifies and validates structure of each type of record maintained by the proposed system
* Performing the following error checks:
* Entry of valid tags
* Proper format as defined for each field (e.g., field length, character type, and numeric range checks.
* Valid entries in controlled fields (from authority lists or files)
* Presence of mandatory data elements.
* Supplies default data element identifiers (tags, indicators, sub field codes, etc.).

Whenever applicable, the Library may specify tags for each template as well as default codes.

The Bibliographic Control/Cataloging module must not require a specific interface to any MARC-based cataloging source. Describe MARC record loading capabilities/utilities within the proposed system.

The Bibliographic Control/Cataloging module must include a utility for verifying uniform resource locator(s), or URLs, cataloged within MARC 856 bibliographic fields. Describe.

The Bibliographic Control/Cataloging module must support creation, editing and maintenance of Community Information records in the MARC Format for Community Information and in a locally developed format.

7.2 Z39.50 MARC Cataloging Client

Bibliographic Control/Cataloging module must include a Z39.50 Copy Cataloging Client that can capture bibliographic records from any Z39.50 bibliographic resource.

The Z39.50 copy cataloging client must capture MARC records from OCLC directly into the Library's catalog, while at the same time updating the Library's holdings on OCLC to reflect the addition of the record.

OCLC and Library of congress provides the facility of copy cataloging. OCLC provides the golden databases "World cat", the world's largest bibliographic databases.

Library of congress is open sources databases

Set the Z39.50 database you wish to obtain records from by selecting databases. Here one example of a Z39.50 databases from which you might obtain records is the Library of Congress. Z39.50 is a International Standard, ISO 23950 and specifies a client/server-based protocol for searching and retrieving information from remote databases.

Library of Congress connection information

Profile Name:	Library of Congress
Description:	Library of Congress
Host Name:	Z3950.loc.gov
Port:	7090
Database:	VOYAGER

Type in the Profile name, Description (name appears in the Connection List box), Host name or IP address of the database, and enter the port number of the database.

After searching the record it can be save to the desktop or directly in databases after proper editing.

7.3 Authority Control

An authority record is a tool librarians use to create forms of names for the persons, places, titles, subjects, etc. that are found in bibliographic records. Authority records provide a controlled vocabulary and cross reference system for accessing bibliographic records.

The Authority Control module must link all authority-controlled bibliographic headings with corresponding authority records through an ANSI-standard thesaurus.

The system's Authority Control module must include a machine-proposed authority feature based upon the Standard for Machine-Proposed Authority Records (http://www.loc.gov/catdir/pcc/strawn.html) developed for the Program for Cooperative Cataloging, which must generate a new authority record with reasonable values in the fixed field and 001, 005, 040, 1XX, and 670 entries (plus the 022 and 642-646 entries for a series heading). These values must be automatically generated based on the information in the bibliographic record being validated. Describe.

The Authority Control module must enable the system administrator to specify whether entry of bibliographic data which does not match an authority record must result in rejection of the input, or in a warning, in which case the system must:

* Display a browse list of possible authority headings from which the operator may choose by clicking the desired heading to replace the unauthorized heading in the bibliographic record
* Automatically flag the unauthorized entry for later display, review, and/or printing

The Authority Control module must support multiple authority files, including separate authority indexes for LC name and subject headings, NLM subjects, or other locally defined indexes.

The Authority Control module must enable the Library to define an unlimited number of authority formats or types, and to specify the bibliographic fields and sub fields addressed by each authority record type through policy configuration.

Vendor must describe the Authority Control module's interactive authority control heading verification process. Describe what the system does when an unauthorized heading is detected?

The Authority Control module must automatically generate appropriate *See* and *See Also* references from authority records for use in the online catalog.

At the Library's discretion, the Authority Control module must be configured either to display cross-references but not to verify headings, or to display cross-references and also to verify headings.

MARC tag of Authority records

Tag	Purpose
1xx	Established Heading: Correct term established by agency (LC, etc.)
3xx	Complex see also references: Defines how term is used. The 360 tag will display as a note in the OPAC.
450	See references: Terms not used. These are cross-references that lead from an unauthorized heading to an authorized heading. They serve as other entry points: see 1xx heading from the 4xx heading.
550	See also references: Terms used to describe similar subjects or alternate names, broader, narrower terms.

	They lead from one authorized heading to another authorized heading. NOTE: Sub-field /w is used to define broader and narrower terms.
68x	Note fields that define the 1xx tag.

7.4 Gift and Legal Deposits

When gifts or legal deposits are received, Software provides a way to both record and acknowledge receipt via the 541 tag of the MARC bibliographic record. The information from the sub fields in the 541 tag are used to generate acknowledgment letters.

Complete the record, using all required fields as well as the 541tag (Immediate Source of Acquisition), which contain additional information needed for the acknowledgment letter.

7.5 Produce Spine and Bar Labels

Software can generate spine and bar code label information to a text file that can then be used with a label program or word processing program to generate labels. This text file can be edited if needed to add or remove data elements. The LabInput.txt file will create a label indicating the location, call number, copy number and bar code (accession number).

Chapter 8
Circulation System

8.1 Circulation Module

The Circulation module must support the following features:

* Full-text search of any word within any bibliographic field
* Circulation functions at a workstation in real time
* Offer an interface with user self-check workstations
* Provide a graphical backup circulation client
* Enable operator to circulate uncaptioned items on-the-fly (e.g., add a brief title, add copies)
* Brief bibliographic records, as well as charging and lending items for interlibrary loans
* Checkout
* Check in
* Renew all items or renew a single item
* Bill a user
* Pay a bill
* Display, create, edit, copy, and remove user record
* Confirm user address
* Renew user privilege
* Send user a message
* Place, edit, display, remove holds
* Claims returned
* Lost card processing
* Modify an item's assigned due date
* Mark item used and inventory item

* Charge ephemeral (impermanent) items
* Book drop check in
* Place and track items in transit (for multi-branch and multi-library systems)
* Circulate items borrowed through ILL once a brief bibliographic record has been created, with local circulation loan parameters determined by a matrix of user profile, item type, and location
* Lend items to ILL partner libraries by creating a user record for each library's ILL department

When an item presented for checkout presents an alert of 'still charged to previous user,' the Circulation Module must allow staff to enter an override password to immediately discharges the item and must allow staff to immediately checkout the material to the present patron.

The Circulation module must sever the link between the item and user at discharge; however, it must be possible for authorized staff to determine the last user to have charged the item until the next user discharges the item, to allow investigation of any damage to items.

The Circulation module must interface seamlessly with other modules, including Cataloging, to enable authorized circulation staff to:

* Add a brief title
* Add copies
* Change item barcode
* Mark item missing or lost
* Remove title, call number/volume or copies

The Circulation module must enable individual user record creation, as well as a patron load utility that allows user records to be imported and updated *en masse.*

When a user who has lost or misplaced his/her library card, the Circulation Module must automatically deactivate the previous library card number and must transfer the user's charges, fines, overdue, holds and bills to the new ID.

8.2 Checkout

* Vendor must describe its circulation policy matrix that allows the Library to define the precise terms under which items can be circulated to users. Circulation policies must be flexible, specific to the Library or to each individual library within a multi-library consortium.
* The Circulation module must support checkout transactions of impermanent materials. These checkout transactions must be recorded for statistical reports and checkout data, but must not be used to generate late notices or bills.

8.3 Check In

* The Circulation module must allow staff to accept payment for fees/bills during item check in (e.g., accept payment for overdue fees) without leaving the discharging process.
* The Circulation module must alert staff and immediately place an item in transit to its home location, if the item is checked in at a location other than its home location.
* The Circulation module must support printing replacement barcodes for damaged item barcodes immediately upon item check in.
* The Circulation module must support the discharge/check in of floating collection materials. When floating items are checked out, then returned, they become a part of the discharging library's collection. The Circulation module must prevent this floating discharge if the item is needed for a hold, booking, or reserve at another library.

8.4 Routing/Transit (For multi-Library Systems)

* The Circulation module must automatically track an item's current and home locations (e.g., Checked out,

ILL, Reference, Bookmobile) and must display these locations for staff and public user searches.

* The Circulation module must permit staff to view items presently in transit to the staff workstations' library (in a multilibrary system) at any time.

8.5 Renewals

* The Circulation module must allow both the renewal of a single item and the renewal of all items charged to a user. Staff and user self-renewal (for selected item(s), and via the web OPAC) must be available.
* The Circulation module must alert staff attempting to renew items for delinquent, blocked, and barred public users. Staff must have the option to investigate or enter an override password to continue with item renewal.
* During renewal, staff must have the option to select a special due date, or to allow the Circulation module to automatically renew according to local library circulation loan policies.

8.6 Fines / Bills

* The Circulation module must support an unlimited number of fine structures, such as hourly and daily. Each fine structure amount may accrue in different rates (fifty centers per unit, two dollars a day, etc.)
* Circulation staff must be capable of displaying all bills within a user record, as well as limiting the display to only bills for items belonging to the staff worker's location. The Circulation module must also enable the display of 'paid' bills.
* The Circulation module must support both automatic, system-generated bills as well as manual, staff-initiated fines. The Circulation module must support an unlimited number of manual fine reasons, including damaged, privilege, hold fee, ILL fee, photocopy.
* The Circulation module must support graduated fines and other billing structures.

* The Circulation module must support the calculation of fines and make this information available to staff and public users (via the user's online OPAC account) prior to check in of items and the creation of a bill.

8.7 Holds /Demand Management (Staff and Public User Placed Holds)

1. The Circulation module must check the validity of the user requesting a hold. The Circulation module must check the user database and block users who are barred, inactive, not permitted to place holds, etc.
2. The Circulation module must examine library-level, group level, and system-wide levels of holds policies. The system must enable a library to allow only its own patrons to place holds on items. In addition, the system must enable a library to assign a higher priority ranking to its users' hold requests (i.e., allow a library to state, 'Fill requests for my library patrons first, then other libraries' users.') The system proposed must allow a definition of one or more groups of libraries that allow reciprocal holds/other library's users to place holds.
3. The Circulation Module must allow holds to be placed:
    * By staff
    * By public users within the library
    * By remote users via the web OPAC
    * At the title or copy level
    * Over a range of materials to fulfill a "blanket hold" request (e.g., any novel by Robert Jordan)
    * Only by authorized users and only on 'hold able' materials as determined by local library circulation policies. For instance, a juvenile cannot place holds on materials, or cannot place holds on materials owned by another library within a multilibrary system
4. For multi-library systems, hold fulfillment policies must consider (a) the user's hold rank and (b) the item's owning

library's policies when determining the next eligible user in the hold queue.

5. Vendor must describe how the proposed Circulation module satisfies user hold requests for any book/item by a particular author or for several items on a specific subject.

8.8 Offline Circulation

1. Vendor must describe the Circulation module's standalone, graphical offline circulation feature.
2. The Circulation module's standalone, graphical PC-based alternative must allow circulation to continue in the event the system cannot be used due to system failure, communications failure, downtime required for maintenance, etc.
3. The offline circulation feature must provide:
   - i. Feature to alert staff when circulating items to blocked users
   - ii. Support for item charge and discharge
   - iii. Renewals
   - iv. Payment collection
   - v. New user registration

8.9 Inventory

* The Circulation module must support marking items 'used' in-house for statistical reporting. If an item has a special status (charged, on hold. in transit), a glossary must appear next to the item for displaying more item information.
* The Circulation module must support the creation of a shelf list from inventory data in report output. Also, staff must be able to list inventory by item number in a report.
* The Circulation module must support the use of portable inventory scanners, provided the Vendor's software is loaded to the Library's portable scanners.

Chapter 9
Serials Control

9.1 Serial Control

A publication in any medium that is issued in successive parts bearing numeric or chronological designations intended to be continued indefinitely. Serials include periodicals; newspapers; annuals (such as reports and yearbooks); the journals, memoirs, proceedings, and transactions of societies; and numbered monographic series.

The serials control module must support the following industry standards:

* SISAC check in with SICI barcode scanning
* MARC21 Format for Holdings Data (MFHD)
* Support but not require MARC Format for Holdings Data (MFHD)
* If the library desires, automatically generate multi-library. holdings data for the 852, 853, 863 and 866 holdings tags
* Holdings record follows the punctuation as described in Z39.71
* Supports NISO Z39.45 Claims for Missing Issues of Serials
* Support NISO Z39.55 Computerized Serials Orders, Claims, Cancellations
* Support NISO Z39.56 Serial Item and Contribution Identifier (SICI)
* Offer interface to third-party binding software application (e.g., LINCPlus)
* Retain the receiving dates for at least 105 most recent issues

* Associate printable copy-specific routing lists with users via the serials control record

The Serials Control module must provide the ability to search for records by:

* Keyword search of every indexed bibliographic field
* Vendor
* Fund number
* Purchase order number
* Location
* System assigned number
* Bibliographic utility assigned number

The Serials Control module must detect and alert operator about duplicates between firm orders and subscription for monographs in series.

9.2 Serials Control Record

* The Library, or each library in a multilibrary system, may maintain its own serials control record. The serials control record must:
    * Designate whether or not to enter copy specific information into the catalog at check in
    * Establish the number of latest issues to display in the OPAC, with an authorized operator able to override this designation at check in
    * Establish custom naming patterns
* Using the serials control record pattern, The Serials Check in and Control module must have the ability to generate predictions, expected issues, for each serial. A prediction record must contain information about a particular issue such as enumeration, chronology, and number of copies expected. At the Library's discretion, predictions may be generated as part of the receipt process once the last predicted issue has been received.
* The system must allow a routing list to be maintained

for each copy of a title to be received and must print a routing list for each copy received. At the time of check in, system must enable an authorized operator to indicate that the routing is not to be activated.

The journals or the periodicals are the most difficult media for handling for a library. Since the journals do not have any specific periodicity and have many issues like the change of frequency , change of name , non receipt of issues. Serials control adheres to the standard MARC 21 Format for Holdings Data and provides functionality for the following tasks:

1. Creating and maintaining holding information
2. Checking in serials
3. Predicting issues
4. Creating routing list
5. Producing reminders
6. Producing and transmitting claims
7. Managing binding tasks

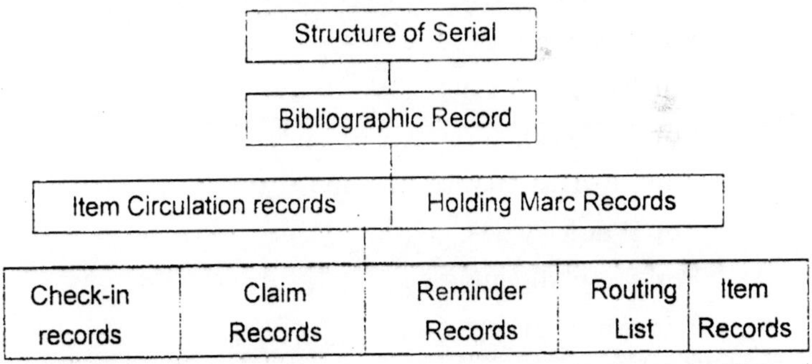

9.2.1 Creating and maintaining holding information

When creating and modifying holding records, the following tags and fields are needed.

Tag 853 for enumeration, chronology and publication pattern sets the stage for the prediction of all expected issues. The fields contains three section of data:

* **Enumeration Captions :** Format labels that display

in the OPAC, e.g., *vol., no.*

* **Chronology Captions :** Specifications as to how often the serial is published, e.g., *weekly, monthly, yearly*
* **Publication Patterns :** Number of issues per year, frequency, when the publication year starts, when the calendar changes)

You would create an 853 tag that looks like this:

853 1# \8 6 \a v.\b no.\u 26\vr\i(year)\j(month)\k (day)\w w \x 01 07

Enumeration and Chronology

In the 853, 854, and 855 tags of enumeration and chronology:

* Six levels of enumeration (stored in sub fields $a - $f)
* Two levels of alternative enumeration (stored in sub fields $g and $h)
* Four levels of chronology (stored in sub fields $i - $l)
* One level of alternative chronology (stored in sub field $m)

List of Allowable Chronology Captions

* **For Year**: year, yr, y
* **For Season**: season, s
* **For Quarter**: quarter, q
* **For Month**: month, mo, m
* **For Week**: week, wk, w
* **For Day**: day, dy, d

Example of an 853 Tag (where ## indicates two indicators):

853 ## \8 6 \a Vol. \b No. \u 12 \v r \i (year) \j (month) \w m \x 01

Example of the Corresponding 863 Tag (generated automatically at check-in of first issue of this serial run for 2002):

863 ## \8 6.1 \a 21 \b 1 \i 2002 \j 01

Supplements and accompanying material. They are defined and stored in 854/864 tags.

Indexes. They are defined and stored in 855/865 tags.

Working with Serials Patterns

Creating accurate serials patterns is a difficult job, some software designed the Serials Pattern Editor to be a convenient tool for working with the complex data in the 853 tag of the holdings record. The Serials Pattern Editor is an easy-to-use interface for generating and editing patterns consisting of basic levels of enumeration and chronology, frequency, and regularity.

About Holdings Record Call Numbers

Your library can choose to include bib-level, holdings-level (852 $h-m), and/or item-level call numbers in the call number index (es). When a holdings-level call number exists, it is taken from a specific sub field of the 852, based on the value of the first indicator of the active 852 tag:

* If the first indicator is 4, $j is used as the call number.
* If the first indicator is 5, $l is used as the call number.
* If the first indicator is any other value, any of the following sub fields that are present are used as the call number: $k, $h, $i, $m.

9.2.2 Checking in serials

Each serials control (check in) record must:

* Be associated with a title in the catalog
* Designate whether or not to enter copy specific information into the catalog at check in
* Establish the number of latest issues to display in the OPAC, with an authorized operator able to override this designation at check in
* Accept the loading of data for titles held by other libraries and not controlled by the system for output in union list products

Record and maintain discard information, for producing automatic discard alerts and instructional slips for disposal of issues

The **Serials Check-In** function was designed to streamline the workflow involved with receiving serials and entering them into the system. While Information on predicted issues can be easily changed to reflect actual dates and other information at the time of check-in, Issue Prediction speeds up the receiving process of predicted arrivals by defaulting most fields. Serials Check-in handles receiving of unpredicted items with equal ease, and include a field where library staff can designate if an item is an issue, a supplement, or an index.

The Serials Check-in window has two tabs: Expected and Received. The Expected tab of the Serial Check-in window displays information about Expected issues. You must add the first issue of any serial manually, regardless of its frequency, using a template that is based on the pattern set up in the 853 tag. Expected issues are two types

The Received tab of the serials Check-in window displays information about issues that are checked in and lets you reverse a check-in for a selected issue.

9.2.3 Predicting issues

Library staff can view and enter publication patterns for serial issues, supplements, and indexes. This information is used by the system to quickly catalogue expected issues of a serial when they are received, and to generate claiming notices when they are not.

Once you add the first regular Expected issue, software can predict future regular issues automatically, or you can add them manually. When the last regular expected issue is checked in, software automatically adds a new Expected issue. The software predicts basic bibliographic units based on the active 853 tag- the 853 tags with the highest link number-of the holding record.

After you check in an Expected issue, it moves to the

Received tab of the Serials Check-in window and is give the status Received. The status of an issue on the Received tab is always received.

Serial issues must exist as Expected issues before they can be checked in/received.

You can add, modify, and delete regular and special Expected issues on the Expected tab of the Serials Check-in window.

* The status of a newly created Expected issue is automatically set to Expected.
* Expected issues can have the status of Expected or Claimed.

You must add the first issue of any serial manually, regardless of its frequency, using a template that is based on the pattern set up in the 853 tag. On the Serials Check-in window, you can add two types of Expected issues:

* **Regular Expected Issues** : Issues that are part of the regular enumeration/chronology sequence of the serial.
* **Special Expected Issues** : Issues that are NOT part of the regular enumeration/chronology sequence of the serial.

Additional *regular* Expected issues are automatically predicted based on the information contained in the active 853 tag and the data in the serial issue template. Special issues are never used to predict the next issue.

In the following sections, we describe in detail how you can add these issues to the list on the Expected tab of the Serials Check-in window.

Once you add the first regular Expected issue, software can predict future issues automatically based on the active 853 tag in the holdings record. Alternatively, you can add future issues manually.

When the last regular Expected issue is checked in, software automatically adds a new Expected issue. The software predicts basic bibliographic units based on the *active*

853 tag¾the 853 tag with the highest link number¾of the holdings record.

Values and dates in predicted issues are incremented as follows:

* The enumeration values, if they exist, are incremented based on the information in the 853 sub fields $a-h, $u, $v, and $x.
* The chronology values, if they exist, are incremented based on the information in the 853 sub fields $i-m, $w, and $y.
* The Expected date is incremented by an interval based on chronology values. If chronology values are not present, the date is incremented based on the publication frequency in the 853, sub field $w.

Working with Gap Issues

A "gap" issue is a serial issue that is checked in out of order, creating a "gap" in the sequence of issues predicted by the system. When the missing issue finally arrives, it can be checked in, but at this point, software checks it in as an "out-of-order" issue, which fills in the gap created by the gap issue.

* Displaying a message to alert you whenever you check in an issue whose enumeration does not match the enumeration of the next Expected issue.
* Creating a new 863 tag when a gap issue is checked in and adding a sub field $w value of "g" to the end of the old 863 tag, i.e., the 863 tag that includes the last issue that was checked in in sequence based on the link and sequence of the 853/863 tags.
* NOT creating a new 863 tag when an out-of-order issue is checked in but instead finding the gap that the issue fills and combining the checked-in issue with data in the 863 tag to close the gap.

Working with Serial Notes

Serials Control supports two types of notes: holding-level

notes and issue-specific notes. **Holding-level notes** are part of the holdings record for a serial and are stored in the 9xx fields. You can view these notes from different access points in the system, but you can add and edit them only via the MARC Editor. **Issue-specific notes** are notes attached to specific issues of a serial. You can create, view, and modify issue-specific notes from the Serials Check-in window.

9.2.4 Creating routing lists

1. The Serials Check in and Control module must support both formal and informal routing lists. Using formal routing, each routed issue is charged to the first user on the associated routing list. As each user returns the issue to a designated point, the issue is discharged and then automatically charged to the next user on the routing list. With informal routing, staff attach printed routing slips to the copy being routed.
2. With formal serials routing, the Serials Check in and Control module must consult each user's priority rank when establishing the order of recipients. Users with higher rank should appear above lowered ranked users within the routing list.
3. The Serials Check in and Control module must be able to maintain separate routing lists for each copy received for a serial.

The **Routing Function** can help libraries manage routing lists. Serials can be routed by a printed list which is produced at the time of check-in. Alternatively, each serial issues can be treated as a circulating item, with a built in reserve list. As each person finishes with the item is it sent to the library to be forwarded to the next person on the list.

A holding routing list is attached to a holdings record and is used to identify a set of patrons who want the serial issues circulated to them. Each patron (or routing destination) on a routing list must have a patron record in the database. Virtua supports both a **holdings routing list** and a **holdings issue routing list**. The holdings issue routing list contains units information for a specific issue and offers a printable format.

In addition to holdings routing lists, software supports patron routing lists, where you can view a list of all the serials that are routed to a particular patron.

A holding routing list indicates the patrons who should receive some or all issues of a serial that have been checked in. In other words, a holdings issue routing list applies to the entire holdings record, not just to a specific serial issue.

Creating and Displaying a Holdings Routing List

For any holdings record, you can create or display a holdings routing list . . .

9.2.5 Producing reminders

Reminder records in Serials Control serve several functions. They let you track 1) new serial titles that have been ordered but not yet received, 2) serial issues that have not arrived by the Expected date, and 3) issues that are claimed but not received by the appropriate date based on specified claim intervals.

Different types of reminders for different situations. There are two main types of reminders:

* Acquisitions Reminders
* Serials Reminders

For Serials reminders, there are three subtypes:

* Check-in Expected Reminders
* Claims Expected Reminders

User-defined Reminders

9.2.6 Working with serial claims

* The Serials Control module must flag items as missing, overdue, duplicate, or to be retained for reconsideration.
* The Serials Control module must enable an authorized operator:

  * To automatically generate claim notices at intervals specified, in printed and machine-readable format
  * To add a claim to the claim list for a title by filling in a screen work form
  * To send as many claims as desired for a missing issue or copy
  * To specify the text of each claim
  * To determine claim action dates by expected receipt dates combined with an operator-specified claim interval
  * To change the claim interval for each title at any time
  * To identify issues requiring second and third claims according to library determined time lags that may be defined for various item types
  * To identify items for which three claims have been issued without a response being recorded, and make them available for staff review to determine further action

* The Serials Control module must enable recording specific details of responses to claims.

Normally, you would use the claiming function in Serials Control to claim a specific Expected issue that has not been received, whereas you would use the claiming function in Acquisitions to claim a new serial order, the first issue of which has not yet arrived.

* **Issue Claims** - Create claims for serials that have not yet been received. You can create a claim either for a specific serial issue or for an entire holdings record.
* **Transmit Claims** - Send claim letters to vendors by means of printing and mailing.
* **View Claims** - See a list of all outstanding claims that have not yet been transmitted.
* **Delete Claims** - Removed from the claims list claims that have not yet been transmitted.

9.2.7 Managing binding tasks

The **Bindery Function** allows library staff to change the material status of serial issues that have been bound into a volume to "Bindery" or its library-defined equivalent. This automatically changes the holdings record and replaces the issues' item records with a single item record for the volume.

Binding control allows your library to manage received journal issues and to track which issues should be sent to the bindery. The features binding control functionality that consists of three main aspects: 1) binding reminders, 2) display on the Serials Check-in window, and 3) a report on those issues to be pulled for binding.

PART IV : AUTOMATED INFORMATION SERVICES

Chapter 10
OPAC/Web OPAC

10.1 OPAC

OPAC stands for Online Public Access Catalogue. It is computer based and supported library catalogue (bibliographic database) designed to be accessed via terminals so that library users may directly and effectively search for and retrieve bibliographic records without the assistance of a human intermediary. OPAC usually allows searching by author name, title, and subject. OPAC proved access to the library's holdings via a computer monitor, replacing the traditional card catalogue.

Features Summary

Online Public Access Catalog must provide searching and locating features for your online public access catalog. Specifically, OPAC offers the following key features:

* Patrons can perform various levels of searching such as Browse, Heading, Keyword, Control number, and Expert.
* Patrons can select which index they wish to search such as title, author, and subject.
* Z39.50 compliance, which allows you to search other Z39.50 compliant databases.
* Patron empowerment such as searching/viewing of own patron record.
* Filtering of searches.
* Browse searches are accumulated on tabs.
* Access to record views such as Full, MARC, Holdings, Item and Status tabs.
* Multimedia access via MARC 856 tag.

Browse Search

The browse search is useful for searching the OPAC when the user wants to narrow a search from a broad topic to a specific topic or does not know an exact term.

Search Strings

* *Author, Instructor, Patron*: Last name first
* *Title*: Do *not* include A, An, The as the first word
* *Subject*: Type the category as it appears in the Library of Congress Subject Headings
* *Course ID searches*: Use the official name and number

View a Record

The **View Record** window provides information about the title/item that was selected from the **List of Titles**. Information concerning the record is displayed on tabs. Different tabs are available for each record type in each different window:

View Bibliographic Record Window

Full tab

Items tab – Access to Item Information windows

MARC tab

Statuses tab – Acquisitions information

Holdings tab - Serials records only

The **Full** tab of the **View Record** window may also contain hyperlinked text.

Multimedia Links: If a bibliographic record is associated with multimedia files (856 tag), the URL of each multimedia file is displayed as a hyperlink.

Search Hyperlinks: The Full tab view may be configured to display the contents of any bibliographic tag as a search hyperlink. When you click the hyperlinked field, Virtua launches a search as specified in the configuration.

Output Records

Copies of bibliographic records can be obtained from the **List of Titles, View Record**, and **MARC Editor** windows in three ways:

1. Print
2. Save
3. Email

Print Record(s)

1. Open the record in the **List of Titles, View Record**, or **MARC Editor** window.
2. Highlight the **Print** option from the File pull-down menu or right click the mouse and select **Print**.

Save Record(s)

1. Open the record in the **List of Titles, View Record**, or **MARC Editor** window.
2. Highlight the **Save** option from the File pull-down menu or right click the mouse and select **Save**; The **Save Records** window will appear.

Email Record(s)

1. Open the record in the **List of Titles, View Record**, or **MARC Editor** window.
2. Highlight the **Email** option from the File pull-down menu or right click the mouse and select **Email**; The **Email Records** window will appear.

Keyword

Keyword searching has the flexibility to allow the user to create simple searches and yet allows the experienced user to build sophisticated searches through Precision Searching and Filtering.

Precision Searching provides enhanced control through expanded keyword search capabilities using the following tools:

* Keywords

* Wild cards
* Phrase searching
* Search Categories (including 008 Fixed Fields)
* Boolean Operators
* Proximity searching
* Parentheses
* Full Text searching

Key Terms

* Boolean Operators
* Filters
* Keyword Search
* Refine
* Search Categories
* Search Strings
* Shelving Location
* Sub-Location

Truncation

With keywords, you can specify left, right, or medial truncation along with wild card searches.

Words truncated with an asterisk (*): Designate one or more characters.

Example Searches	Retrieves
farm*	farm, farms, farming, or other words starting with farm.
Wa*n	walton, warden, Washington, etc.

Boolean Operators & Search Operators

Boolean operators (symbols) or Search Operators (terms), are used to link two or more keywords. In Virtua, these operators are available on drop-down menus or can be used within the text boxes as part of search string. If entering them as part of a search string, you must put a space before and after each operator and use a symbol such as & or +.

Symbols	Terms
&	AND
+	OR
-	AND NOT
&x	NEAR: Proximity, where x is the number of words between the search terms, for example: t:Gone &2 wind will retrieve Gone with the Wind.

Parentheses

You can use parentheses anywhere within a query string to group a set of operators and search terms. Search strings within the parentheses will be processed first and then those results will be combined with other terms.

Use the plus (+) and minus (-) signs to include or exclude search terms from your group:

Example Search	Retrieves
(art history) – art, greek	Records that have *art* AND *history* as a subject but do not have *art, Greek* as a subject are found.

Use the plus (+) and minus (-) signs within groups:

Example Search	Retrieves
(t:painting + art) & a:mayer	Records that have *painting* in the title AND *art* as a subject AND *Mayer* as an author are found.

Use nested logic that combines two sets of terms using two sets of parentheses:

Example Search	Retrieves
((art or sculpture) & art collections)	Records that have *art* OR *sculpture* as subjects AND *art collections* are found.

Proximity Searching

Bibliographic keyword searches let you specify proximity between search terms using either the **NEAR** operator that appears in the search operators pull-down list box or with the **&xx** operator. The value of the **x** indicates the number of words between the two terms. For example, **&3** indicates proximity of three words.

Example Search	**Retrieves**
t:ancient &1 t:rome	Records in which *ancient* appears within one word of *Rome* in any indexed title field are found.

Search Categories

When specifying a search category, type the category code, followed by a colon and the search term. Do ***not*** put a space between the category code and the colon or the colon and the search term.

Example Search	**Retrieves**
a: Bronte	Records authored by Bronte, Charlotte; Bronte, Emily; etc. are found.

Control Number Search

Control numbers are unique numbers assigned to library items or attached to catalog records and subsequently are used to identify those items or records.

Key Terms

* Authority MARC Record
* Control Number
* Control Number Search
* Holdings MARC Record
* Item Record
* Patron Record

Vendor Record

Control Numbers and Search Results

Index	*Searches*	*Retrieves*
Auth ID	001 tag of the MARC Authority record.	View (Authority) Record window
Bib ID	001 tag of the MARC Bibliographic record	View (Bibliographic) Record window
ISBN	020 tag of the MARC Bibliographic Record	View (Bibliographic) Record window
ISSN	022 tag of the MARC Bibliographic Record	View (Bibliographic) Record window
LCCN	010 tag of the MARC Bibliographic Record	View (Bibliographic) Record window
OCLC #	035 tag of the MARC Bibliographic Record	View (Bibliographic) Record window
Local #	Searches the exact content of the 035 of the MARC Bibliographic Record tag as opposed to the OCLC search that searches the OCLC number and automatically adds the (OCoLC)ocm prefix.	View (Bibliographic) Record window
Vendor #	System-generated Vendor ID number	View Vendor window
Patron Barcode	015 of the Patron Record	Patron Information window
Patron ID	001 of the Patron Record	Patron Information window
Holdings ID		001 tag of the Holdings Record View Holdings window
ISSN Serials	022 tag of the MARC Bibliographic Record	Serials Check-in window
Item Barcode	Item barcode number	Item Information window
Item ID	System ID number of the Item Record	Item Information window
Auth Ctrl #	010 tag of the Authority Record	View (Authority) Record window

10.2 Web OPAC

10.2.1 Broadcast Searching

Broadcast searching option that can be integrated with Vendor's web OPAC to enable users to conduct simultaneous searches across both Z39.50 and non-Z39.50 targets including:

* Commercial abstract and index databases,
* Library catalogs,
* Search engines (like Google, Teoma, etc.)
* Speak to each source in its native language to provide superior results.
* Keep access to resources reliable with continuous updates through subscription-based Resource Plugging
* Deliver results merged into a single interface to enable users to limit searches, sort, reduplicate, and filter.

10.2.2 Open URL resolution

Open URL Resolve must resolve an Open URL initiating with the vendor's proposed web OPAC, or with third-party Open URL products, such as Ebsco HOST, etc., to identify and retrieve information related to the original citation, even though such information may be scattered among different providers.

Open URL Resolve must return and resolve, wherever available, information from:

* Full-text document databases
* Abstract and index databases
* Citation databases
* Content databases with reviews, tables of contents, first chapters, summaries, author biographies, etc.
* Online library catalogs – both local and remote
* Interlibrary loan and document delivery services
* Web sites
* Electronically accessible resources of all kinds free or licensed, to which the library has access.

10.3 Web Report

* The Reports module must be fully integrated with all other system modules, and provide a comprehensive suite of library-customizable report templates.
* The Reports module must enable an authorized operator to schedule production of report output at a specified date and time and on a regular periodic basis, such as daily, weekly, monthly, and at pre-specified times.
* The Reports module must enable an authorized operator to view completed reports on screen or to e-mail or print the report, at the operator's convenience.
* On any database reports involving materials, such as new accessions lists, shelf lists, high/low circulation lists, and bibliographies, the operator can select items for inclusion based on any combination of bibliographic information (using full Boolean word and phrase searching) and on any combination of control information, for example collection, current status, number of circulations, number of holds, classification, and accessions date.
* The Reports module must enable an authorized operator to specify the starting date-and-time and ending date-and-time that the report is to cover on reports involving historical data.
* The fully integrated Reports module must use the same user interface as other modules. The Reports module must:
    * Provide lists, counts, and statistical reports for each purchased module
    * Provide row, column, and grand totals in applicable reports
    * Provide reports for all record types within the proposed system
    * Track statistical and management information by counting various staff processes to measure

productivity, identifying items which are likely candidates for weeding, or tracking fund information for budgeting

* Perform housekeeping tasks by changing the status of groups of users, or removing users or items in batches when necessary
* Allow authorized operator(s) to select, customize, name, save and schedule reports
* Allow staff to display and/or e-mail finished reports

10.4 What is Z39.50?

Z39.50 is an international standard for communication protocol, which specifies data structures, and interchange rules that allow a client machine to search databases on a server machine and retrieve records that are identified as a result of such a search.

Z39.50 is becoming increasingly important to the future development and deployment of inter-linked library systems.

Implications for libraries

The implications for the library and information services are profound. Over the next few years, services will become "Z39.50 enabled" in much the same way that library OPACs have become "Web enabled". Some possible effects on library operations are explored here:

OPACs

Many OPACs have been Z39.50 for a few years now. This is the basic benefit of Z39.50 operation for a typical user.

The typical (simplified) search process involved in a Z39.50 session is as follows:

* OPAC user selects Target library (Z-server) from an OPAC menu.
* OPAC user enters search terms
* OPAC software sends search terms and Target library details to a "Z-client" a piece of software usually running as part of the library system.

* Z-client translates the search terms into "Z-speak" and contacts the Target library's Z-server software.
* There is a preliminary negotiation between the Z-client and Z-server to establish the rules for the "Z-Association" between the two systems.
* Z-server translates the "Z-speak" into a search request for the Target library's database and receives a response about numbers of matches etc.
* Z-client receives records
* Records are presented to the OPAC interface for the user.

Cataloguing

Searching for and downloading bibliographic records using a Z39.50 tool is simple and very efficient since multiple sources can be searched simultaneously and records easily compared. The cataloguing process involved in a Z39.50 session is as follows:

* Modern Z-clients can send requests to several libraries simultaneously either the same request or different ones. This feature allows tremendous time saving when searching for rare items or for large numbers of records.
* The basic record format used for interchange is MARC. The Z-client is presented with a MARC record for display and possible further processing. All libraries "trade" in bibliographic records one way or another. Z39.50 opens up that trade by making standardising the basic search and retrieve functions.

Union catalogues

Union catalogues - combined catalogues of several libraries - have been a valuable tool for decades within groups of otherwise separate libraries wanting to co-operate for inter-lending, co-operative purchase, and general reader service. They are, however, difficult and expensive to manage. Using Z39.50 enabled catalogues and OPACs, a "virtual" union catalogue can be assembled without any changes to the individual organization's methods and procedures. A user may sit at an OPAC screen and search several catalogues simultaneously as if they were one. Useful material and its location can be displayed with no additional work by library management apart from set-up of Z-clients. Ad-hoc groupings of libraries can be assembled to suit the needs of the users without any technical or administrative fuss.

Inter-Library Loan (ILL)

The immediate benefit of a virtual union catalogue means that ILL is made easier the user can immediately identify the location of required items. The extended services of Z39.50 allows systems to arrange for the delivery, including account verification and billing, of an item to the enquirer. In a Z39.50 enabled ILL future, libraries will be able to search and order items in one operation and deal directly with whichever library serves their needs all via their own library OPAC search tools.

CD-ROM access

Despite the steady migration of CD-ROM information providers to Web based services, CD networks will be a feature of library services for some time. Using Z39.50, it would be possible to search each database using a single familiar interface and, additionally, several databases at the same time.

Selective Dissemination of Information

Z39.50 allows the user to specify search statements to be saved and run at intervals. Thus the user may for instance identify useful libraries and information resources and set up SDI profiles using a single interface. Searches can be automatically run when required and the results downloaded from the database to a specified destination e.g. fax or e-mail.

Chapter 11
Extended Services

11.1 Extended Services

Automated library provides extended services to satisfy the needs of the users. Some of the services which most of the university libraries provide are:

11.1.1 Reservation service

In case a document has been loaned, then a user, who needs it, can get it reserved. So that when the document is returned then the user can be informed and he/she can get it issued. Online reservation facility should be there as many users need not come to the library to reserve a book, in that case online reservation facility helps them a lot.

11.1.2 Reference service

Reference Service is the hub of all the activities of a library. Reference service is ' a sympathetic and informed personal aid in interpreting library collection for study and research'. Samuel Rothstein gave the following distinguishing criteria of reference service.

The provision by librarians of personal assistance to individual readers in pursuit of information.

The recognition by the library that such assistance is an indispensable means of a definite responsibility to provide it. The existence of a specific administrative unit to furnish such assistance comprised of personnel specially equipped in the techniques of reference work.

According to Dr. Ranganathan, "Reference Service is the achievement of modern humanism in library science and it is a contact between the right reader and the right book at the right time and in the right personal way".

The objectives of Reference Services are:

* Providing of information using reference books in response to specific queries of the users.
* Giving instructions in the use of, and guidance in the choice of documents.
* Giving referral service for inquires which the information centre/ system cannot answer.

According to Dr. S. R. Ranganathan there are following four kinds of reference service.

These are

* Initiation of the freshman.
* General help to the general reader
* Short-range Reference Service.
* Long-range Reference Service.

Initiation of the freshman

When a new reader becomes a member of the library he is initiated into the technicalities of the library and large stock of the library. If he is left totally unnoticed, there is a danger that he may feel bewildered and may not be able to use the library resources. It is essential to create confidence in him so that he uses the library without doubt or fear. He should be properly guided as to the location of various kinds of books. He should be told the method of finding out the requisite reading material. Readers of this kind should be fully guided as to how to become a member of the library and to use its resources.

General help to the General Reader

Readers of this kind are not new to the library but they still want some kind of help so that they may be able to get their requisite reading materials. They must be told as to how to use the catalogue and various sequences of the library. It means that such readers do not ask any particular question but they would like to know the methods of using the library resources in a better way.

Short-Range Reference Service

Short-range Reference Service consists of providing readymade answers to particular questions. Time is the essence of his kind of service. No special effort is to be made to find out the requisite information.

Long-range Reference Service

This kind of service is just the reverse of short-range reference service. To cull out information, lot of time has to be devoted and the sources from which information is got out are not ready reference books but lengthy reports and treaties, which need, prolonged search for finding out the adequate and proper information.

11.1.3 Referrel service

Normally reference staff attempts to bring users in contact with documents likely to contain required information. Similarly reference staff can tell about the persons and institutions, which may be able to provide information to the users seeking information.

11.1.4 Indexing and abstracting service

Indexing and abstracting, which follow preliminary selection and acquisition of documents, involve the process of assigning descriptors to each document to identify the data or information. This would involve a comprehensive and highly condensed presentation of information. This results in indexing and abstracting services/ products that indicate to a user the type of data/ information contained as well as parameters of data points. Some of the products emanating from these services are, Abstracts of technical papers, Patent abstracts, Digest for management, Digest for technical division, Digest for operator, technical note etc.

11.1.5 Current awareness service (CAS)

Current awareness services are a good way to track recent developments on a specific topic or keep up-to-date in a specific field of interest. It supports your research, teaching and studies is vital in this information intensive Internet age. It is essential that users manage the amount of information using a range of current awareness services. Following types of current awareness services:

* **Electronic Table of Contents (TOC) Service**

Electronic Tables of Contents service is provided by the Library to keep you up to date with the latest articles and information in your specialty. It contains the title, author, journal name, inclusive page numbers etc. ISBN, Elsevier, Sage publication, SARA, ACS, Springer and many other publisher are providing this types of services.

* **SDI (Selective Dissemination of Information) Service**

H.P.Luhn is a pioneer in this field. According to him, " SDI is that service within an organization which concerns itself with channeling of new items of information from various sources to those points within the organization where they can usefully serve someone's interest. It endeavors to prevent indiscriminate distribution of new information and avert the resulting danger of not communicating at all". The basic concept behind SDI consists of matching information/ documents with the profile (interest) of each individual of the clientele. The profile can be single user or a group working on the same project or some limited subject field. Those item matches are brought to the attention of the user. In an automated system this service can be performed effectively. The aim being that user should neither be provided too much information nor made to miss information essential towards his requirements. The steps involved here are:

* Users Profile,
* Documents Profile,
* Matching,
* Notification,
* Response or Feedback,
* Readjustment or rejuvenation of Profiles

* **Electronic Clipping Services**

This service identifies news as it is added to the database. The user is prompted to indicate the files to be monitored, the search strategies to be used and the name of resulting "folder". Each folder can have upto five search statements. User is asked to specify the delivery options for the clippings. The user has the option to review the headlines of the clipped articles before viewing the full-text. Clippings are kept in a folder for 30 days if not deleted by the user before then. It can be delivered by fax or email.

* **Publications**

Publications of the library or of the parent institutions can be on the Web page. Many universities having printing press and publication division. If the library has an independent Web page along with that of the institute, a link may be provided to the publication's page. Alternatively, the library can maintain in its Web page information about the university publications.

11.1.6 Supporting services

The supporting services include

* **Translation Service**

The non-English language potion of the world's scientific and technical literature required by scientists, engineers, and technologists probably amounts to as much as 50 percent. At present, the most expedient way to make this body of foreign language material available to the scientists and engineers of the system is by the provision of a translation facility.

* **Reprography Service**

The art and method of document reproduction broadly defined as "Reprographic Methods", have come to stay as a basic necessity in every aspect of modern life, more so in the field of communication and dissemination of information.

The advantage of reprography has found innumerable applications in information centres and their scope is practically unlimited. The advantages are:

* Procuring copies of out-of-print material or unpublished works such as laboratory notes;
* Securing the contents of valuable documents;
* Publication in limited editions;
* Saving storage space;
* Acquisition of copies of portions of books, periodicals, etc. without having to acquire the whole of the original etc.

* Printing Service

Apart from providing access to documents by the supply of copies, the reprography unit would also be bringing out the abstracting periodicals, current awareness services, cover-to-cover translations and other information publications. It may also be required to bring out the organizations Technical Journal, Conference Seminar and Symposia papers, Proceedings etc. Therefore, printing facilities are required to be set up. In a computer-oriented automated environment the lithography system can make use of computer printout directly.

* Instruction Service

This service can also be called as User Education. This service aims to provide knowledge and skills necessary to find out his own way. The objectives of user education are:

* A general orientation to available facilities and resources
* The teaching of basic research skills and strategies and
* The teaching of the organization of the literature in various disciplines, as well as basic reference tools in each discipline.

Thus the achievement of the objectives will facilitates recognition on the part of users of their own information needs as formulation of those needs.

The user education constituted of the four interrelated components. These are

* User awareness,
* Library orientation,
* Interest profiling,
* Bibliographic instruction.

Once users have been made aware of the library as a primary source of information, then they must be oriented of library facilities. Thus user awareness is the initial stage, preceding library orientation. Interest profiling should precede bibliographic instruction. Library orientation and bibliographic instruction form the basic components of user education. Library orientation precedes bibliographic instruction. Library orientation is supposed to lay groundwork for bibliographic instruction whereby the users can become effective users.

11.1.7 Bulletin board service

Very often, researchers and academicians need to discuss their individual findings and study with fellow academicians. The quickest and easiest way of doing this would be to have a type of Discussion Forum or Bulletin Board Service on the Internet, which would be a kind of bulletin board for members to "pin their notes" for others to see. Generally Bulletin Board Service is used to invite people's interest in special resources and services: to house interests in selected books on a particular topic; to present short, graphic summaries of important national and local news; and to announce programs and lectures. The bulletin boards should be installed in places where too many readers come.

11.1.8 CD-ROM service

CD-ROM is a high capacity storage media, which is widely used in libraries due to its various advantages. Libraries store different reference books as they take lots of space on the shelf and also because of their heavy weights. Different abstracting and indexing journals are now available on CD-ROM, for example, LISA (Library and Information Science Abstract), ISA (Indian Science Abstract), etc. The libraries those have infrastructure to use CD-ROM provide this service to the users. It is a way of providing bibliographic services using CD-ROM. Another reason of libraries using CD-ROM is that some documents are available in CD-ROM. To give access to those books libraries provide CD-ROM service.

11.1.9 Online book suggestion

This is a good service usually offered by the university. One can suggest a book for the library to acquire via e-mail. For this the person in charge of this matter should have e-mail facility. The user should provide the following items of the documents to be acquired.

* The name and department of the user who is suggesting.
* The status of the user (e.g. undergraduate, graduate, faculty, staff) with e-mail address.
* For each item suggested, one should provide Author (required), Title (required), Publisher, Year of publication, Price, ISBN number.

11.1.10 Shared cataloging

Even when using CIP or one of the CD-ROM or Web-based cataloging products, smaller libraries seldom have adequate time or other resources available to maintain consistently high quality cataloging. In a shared system this cataloging can be much easier, saving a considerable amount of time and money. For example, if five libraries in the shared system purchase the same title, only one library has to actually catalog it. Once a title is cataloged, other libraries can simply enter their holdings data, such as the call number and collection code ("Ref," "Juv," etc.). The benefits of not having to catalog most acquisitions, nor file catalog cards for them, can be significant.

PART V : TECHNOLOGICAL TRENDS IN LIBRARY

Chapter 12
Digitalization System

12.1 Digitalization System

Digital libraries are revolutionizing the way institutions can store, organize and deliver information. The first responsibility of a digital library system is that it manages the electronic assets in a way that provides maximum security while providing flexible, appropriate levels of access to everything in our collection. It must also do as much as possible to ease the task of maintaining the storage and archiving of the assets.

The data model for the digital objects is crucial to the design of the entire system. Essentially, each digital object is a free agent in the system, carrying all of the information needed to understand and use it. E-texts, images, collections, etc. are all represented as independent objects in the system, as are thesauri, union lists, indices and other types of information structures. The repository architecture must be able to completely implement the data model for objects that are not resident on our systems as well as for those that are. For objects that are not ours but for which we are acting as the primary gateway, the repository should be able to maintain the metadata package and methods for each object and the registry should be able to uniquely identify it. We should be able to create our own behaviors for the remote objects that make them usable in our system.

12.2 What is a Digital Library?

Digital libraries emerged from research and development activities in the decade of the 1990s. For Duguid, a digital library is "an environment to bring together collections, services, and people in support of the full life cycle of creation, dissemination, use, and preservation of data, information, and knowledge." This definition seems particularly appropriate for a higher education community attempting to balance the flexibility of virtual space with the power that physical space brings to the learning process.

Definition

"The concept behind Digital Libraries (DL) has its roots in what is the philosophy of libraries of disseminating 'knowledge for all" — *H.G. Wells*

"Digital libraries are organizations that provide the resource including the specialized staff, to select structure, offer intellectual access to, interpret, distribute, preserve the integrity of, and ensure the persistence over time of collections of digital works so that they are readily and economically available for use by a defined community or set of communities"

— *Donald Waters*

"Controlled collections of information bearing objects (IBOs) that are in digital form and that may be organized, accessed, evaluated and used by means of heterogeneous and extensible set of distributed services that are supported by digital technology" — *Terence R. Smith*

"System providing a community of users with coherent access to a large, organized repository of information and knowledge. The digital library is not just one entity, but multiple sources are seamlessly integrated."

—*Clifford Lynch*

12.3 Packaged DL Software

* E- Prints from the University of Southampton
* Dspace from the Massachusetts Institute of Technology & HP alliance team
* Greenstone from University of Waikato
* Fedora from University of Verginia and Cornell University
* VITAL

NDLTD project has international members from over dozen countries sharing electronic theses and dissertations. Eventually this will become one of the world's largest digital libraries, with the potential of 200,000 multilingual hypermedia works being added each year.

NSDL The basic objective of NSDL is to catalyze and support continual improvements in the quality of Science, Mathematics, Engineering and Technology education.

12.3.1 Dspace

Dspace is open source software for building and managing Digital repositories. Developed jointly by MIT Libraries and Hewlett-Packard (HP), is freely available to research institutions as an open source system that can be customized and extended. Dspace is a digital institutional repository that captures, stores, indexes, preserves, and redistributes content in digital formats. Institutional Respositry is a set of services that a research institution/ organization/ university offers to the members of its community for the management and dissemination of digital materials created by the institution and its community members Typically, Dspace has been deployed for Institutional Repositories of publication, thesis and dissertations. There are several groups working on extending its capabilities such implementation of ontologies in search interface and for submission module, customization for management of electronic theses and dissertations and for localization and international of the package for the world languages.

DSpace is designed for ease-of-use, with a web-based user interface that can be customized. The DSpace system provides a way to manage research materials and publications in a professionally maintained repository to give them greater visibility and accessibility over time.

12.3.2 Fedora from University of Verginia and Cornell University

The *F*lexible and *E*xtensible *D*igital *O*bject and

*R*epository *A*rchitecture (*Fedora*™) system, designed by the *Cornell Digital Library Research Group*, showed great promise as the core architecture of a digital repository system when we first reviewed it in a *1999 D-Lib article*. The University of Virginia Library' s Digital Library Research and Development Group (DLR&D) is collaborating with Cornell to develop Fedora under a $1,000,000 *Andrew W. Mellon Foundation grant*, which has also funded a $1,400,000 *Fedora Phase 2 grant*.

In the first phase of the project, UVa implemented a prototype repository based on the Fedora™ architecture (*see the July 2000 D-Lib Magazine article*) using a relational database combined with Java servlets that provide a web interface. The first phase UVa production repository is scheduled to launch in 2004. Fedora™ is intended to leave a great deal of room for a repository to develop to serve local needs while providing enough structure to guarantee interoperability with other repositories. See *Building an American Studies Information Community* to read a description of a Mellon-funded project that is developing collections and disseminator prototypes for the UVa Repository, and visit the first phase *American Studies Information Community*. Version 1.0 was released under on May 16, 2003.

VTLS, Inc. has announced the release of VITAL, which provides "VTLS developed workflow extensions, management utilities and enhanced searching capabilities" built on top of the Fedora repository system architecture.

12.3.3 VITAL

VITAL provides all types of information is not only transmitted by words—but also by photographs, slides, maps, posters, and videos, sound and movie —just to name a few. By incorporating these into your digital collections, you are providing the public with a rich, new source of information to explore. The following features of the VITAL:

* Instant access to digital content anytime, from anywhere, to anyone with a web browser
* Tools to facilitate the digitization of all materials including, rare objects or historical documents
* Simultaneous access to diverse content and metadata through Fedora™ digital objects

12.4 Digital Image Capture

Digital image capture divides the image into a grid of tiny regions, each of which is represented by a digital value which records color information. The resolution of the image indicates how densely packed these regions are and is the most familiar measure of image quality. However, in addition to resolution you need to consider the bit-depth, the amount of information recorded for each region and hence the possible range of tonal values. Scanners record tonal values in digital images in one of three general ways: black and white, grayscale, and color. In black and white image capture, each pixel in the digital image is represented as either black or white (on or off). In 8-bit grayscale capture, where each sample is expressed using 8 bits of information (for 256 possible values) the tonal values in the original are recorded with a much larger palette that includes not only black and white, .but also 254 intermediate shades of gray. In 24-bit color scanning, the tonal values in the original are reproduced from combinations of red, green, and blue (RGB) with palettes representing up to 16.7 million colors.

12.5 Digital Text Capture

Although it may seem odd to discuss digital text in this context, there are some important, if indirect parallels between the principles described above and those that govern digital text capture. Clearly in capturing digital text one does not sample the original in the same way that one samples audio or images. However, the process of text capture does involve choices about the level of granularity at which the digital representation will operate. In capturing a 20th-century printed text, for instance, a range of different "data densities" is possible: a simple transcription of the actual letters and spaces printed on the page; a higher-order transcription which also represents the nature of textual units such as paragraphs and headings; an even more dense transcription which also adds inferential information such as keywords or metrical data. Other possibilities arise in texts that have different kinds of internal granularity. In the case of a medieval manuscript, one might create a transcription that captures the graphemes—the individual characters—of the text but does not distinguish between different forms of the same letter (for instance, short and long s). Or one might capture these different letter forms, or even distinguish between swashed and unswashed characters. One might also choose to capture variations in spacing between letters, lines of text, and text components, or variations in letter size, or changes in handwriting, or any one of a number of possibly meaningful distinctions.

These distinctions, and the choice of whether or not to capture them, are the equivalent of sampling rates and bit-depth: they govern the amount of information which the digital file records about the analog source, and the resulting amount of nuance that is possible in reusing and processing the digital file.

12.6 Equipment for Digitization

12.6.1 Computers

Computer hardware and software is constantly changing. Fortunately, currently produced computers are fast enough to handle almost any scanning and other digitization tasks. Here are some minimum guidelines for computer hardware:

Pentium III or IV 800 Mhz or better

iMac or Power Mac G4 600 Mhz or better

RAM-intensive operations such as image processing and video editing can take many seconds or even minutes in computers with dozens, rather than hundreds or even thousands of MB of memory. Design a test sequence to allow you to determine whether the machine will achieve your objectives.

256 Megs of Ram or more

Large hard drive (20+ Gigabytes)

CD-R or CD-RW Drive

CD-ROM Drive (for copying CD media)

Zip Drive

12.6.2 Display devices

Large Monitor (19 inch or larger)

Do not neglect display where image work is concerned. Your computer display is likely to be the most used output device and a good quality display of sufficient size is important for effective and efficient quality control and comfortable working conditions. The display should ideally be 19" or 21" inch diagonal viewable measurement. Upgrading to a 21" display is a worthwhile investment. If the monitor is to be used for rigorous quality control ("soft proofing"), ensure that the display has hardware and/or software calibration, that the calibration mechanisms are compatible with the capture devices, and that standard color management profiles can be used. It is also important to control or calibrate the ambient environment along with the display device. If you are considering LCD flat panel monitors, they are available with analog or digital signal processors. The digital signal displays are better but not always compatible with all systems and video cards, so research the hardware carefully.

Printers

Printer resolution is a measure of the printer's ability to produce individual dots, and is usually expressed as dots per inch (dpi). Printer resolution may also be expressed as lines per inch (Dpi).

The variables of paper, ink, storage environment, and

use all determine the life expectancy of their output.

12.6.4 Audio equipment

Film can be transferred onto videotape for digitization via a transfer box or multiplexer. Both of these options depend upon the material being projected in some way. Transfer boxes project the image into a box containing a mirror and onto a rear image projection screen with the video camera mounted on the other side of the box. The resulting video is subsequently digitized. These transfer boxes are not expensive, but do not in general produce quality as high as a multiplexer because they introduce generational loss.

A better solution is to use a multiplexer. In this device the projector and camera are mounted on a single table. The image is projected by a set of lens and mirrors, directly into the camera without the need for a projection screen. This has advantages for image clarity. In both processes quality suffers because it introduces an extra production generation into the reformatting of the analog material.

As there are fewer analog audio formats, these provide less of a problem than moving images. Compact cassette players, 33 and 45 rpm record players are still widely available new. Even record players with a 78 rpm speed can still be purchased new. The other formats present a greater challenge. If digitizing the sound as played on period equipment is important the tone arms of phonographs and gramophones can be customized to provide an appropriate feed.

12.7 Storage Devices and Systems

While storage devices have grown steadily since their invention and show no signs of reaching a plateau, storage demands have kept pace with them, and file storage remains a concern for delivery and for backup. Consider that 150 24-bit color TIFF files at 400 pixels per inch (ppi), plus 150 JPEG files at 100 ppi, together with associated metadata, would occupy 5 - 6 GB. In 2002, this is approximately the entire capacity of most standard PC internal hard drives.

12.8 Software

For most scanning applications, Adobe Photoshop is the de facto standard and is recommended. Photoshop is more expensive than some other imaging packages, but the quality of images produced by Photoshop has been shown to be greater than those produced by other software.

Scanners also come with a driver application that operates the scanner and sends the image to Photoshop. The features included in these applications are dependent on the scanner manufacturer, but they usually include the ability to preview, descreening functionality for halftone (dot-based) images, and color correction.

12.9 Scanning

The process for scanning documents is:

Create a master image, saved as a TIFF (Tagged Image File Format) File Generate derivative or access images from this master image save the master images onto CD-R disks and mount the access images on a web server for public access

For **manuscripts and printed materials** use the following guidelines:

300 dpi minimum

24-bit RGB color

Sharpen lightly if needed using unsharp mask filter (be careful not to use too much!)

12.10 Cropping

Cropping depends on the material being scanned. For most images, any background is cropped out leaving just the object. Photographs can be cropped to the edges of the photograph, and printed books can be cropped to the edge of the page. It is desirable for items such as diaries to crop outside the edge of the object, so that your image looks like a picture of a book rather than disembodied pages.

12.10.1 Image derivatives

Several common types of derivative images may be created from master images.

GIF (Graphics Interchange Format) This format is only currently used for creating thumbnails and 1 bit bitonal (black & white) images.

JPEG (Joint Photographic Experts Group) This format is widely used for creating medium and high resolution images for Web delivery.

PDF (Portable Document Format) From Adobe, this compressed format requires users to have the Adobe Acrobat Reader software installed on their machine (a common default on newer machines and browsers). It offers the benefit of re-sizing on screen and easy printing of documents. This format is most commonly used for printed documents.

12.12 Text Encoding

Documents, books, and other written and printed materials may also be transferred into text format as part of the digitization process. This can be done either through OCR (Optical Character Recognition) Technology or by hand transcription, commonly called "rekeying."

Because text transcription and encoding is very expensive and time consuming, individual projects will want to consider whether or not to make the investment. If the documents have high historical value and searchability is an important criteria of digitization, then transcription and encoding are the preferred method of achieving this goal.

12.13 What is metadata?

Metadata is literally "information about the data": information created about the source material and the digital version to record the essentials of their identity, creation, use, and structure. Their purpose is to facilitate the discovery, use, management and reusability of digital material. Metadata can be usefully divided into three categories: descriptive, administrative and structural. These are not rigidly bounded groups and they frequently overlap.

Descriptive metadata describes and identifies information resources, to facilitate searching, retrieval, and management. It typically includes basic bibliographic information such as the creator, title, creation date; catalog information such as accession or other identifying numbers; and topic information such as keywording. Examples of descriptive metadata include Library of Congress Subject Headings, Categories for the Description of Works of Art (CDWA) and the Dublin Core metadata set.

Administrative metadata is used to facilitate management, tracking, migration and re-use of digital assets. It typically includes information on creation, quality control, rights and preservation. See Cornell University's "Web Hub for Developing Administrative Metadata for Electronic Resource Management"

The term "technical metadata" is also used in a similar sense to indicate metadata about data capture and the technical characteristics of the images.

Structural metadata describes the internal structure of digital resources and the relationships between their parts. It is used to enable navigation and presentation

12.13.1 Text metadata

Metadata for textual resources is in some ways the most straightforward to create, because it can be captured in the same format as the digital object itself, and can be included directly in the digital file, for instance as a header section in an SGML/XML-encoded document. EAD, TEI, and HTML all include a header element of varying scope; the HTML header provides for the inclusion of basic Dublin Core metadata terms, while the EAD and TEI headers provide for more extensive information about both the electronic file and the information it captures or describes.

12.13.2 Image metadata

Metadata for still images may be stored in a file header or in a separate database or file. Because images themselves, unlike text, cannot currently be searched very effectively for content, metadata is doubly important for retrieval purposes, as well as for internal project tracking, management, and documentation. The METS standard can be used to bring together the different types of image metadata required for different project purposes. It can also be used not only to document individual images, but also to represent the relationships between multiple images that together constitute a single digital object (for instance, high-resolution archival images, thumbnails and delivery images at lower resolutions, images of particular details at higher magnification).

12.13.3 Audio-visual metadata

As with still images, metadata is crucial to digital audio or video, and the principles of metadata interoperability and documentation standards are as important to digital AV media as to still image and text media. Metadata for digital audio and visual resources can be used in much the same way as metadata for complex digital objects composed of still images. A metadata standard like METS (with the appropriate extension schema) can be used to describe the structure of an audio-visual digital object: for instance, a group of original taped interviews and a final version edited for delivery.

12.14 Dublin Core

The Dublin Core Metadata Element Set defines a set of 15 essential metadata components:

* **Title:** The title of the item or resource.
* **Creator:** The creator of the item, in Library of Congress authority.
* **Subject:** Subjects covered by the item. Use of controlled vocabularies such as Library of Congress Subject Heading.
* **Description:** A short description of the item.

* **Publisher:** Enter the name of the repository where the original materials are held.
* **Identifier:** Filename, image number, PURL, or other URI (Uniform Resource Identifier) for the image.
* **Date**

The date the image or transcription was created. Note the date of the creation of the material goes in "Coverage."

* **Coverage(Temporal)**

The date of the creation of the material in the form YYYY-MM-DD. So for a letter written on November 20, 1864, enter the date as 1864-11-20.

Coverage (Spatial)

The name of the Georgia county and/or city in which the item originated. If none is indicated, "Georgia" will be sufficient. Use Kenneth K. Krakow, *Georgia Place Names: Their History and Origins* 2nd ed. (Macon: Winship Press, 1994), and the *Thesaurus of Geographic Names* where possible for a controlled list. If from another state, list the city, county, and state as available.

* **Format**

The format of the image or digital file, expressed in the *MIME format*. For example: image/tiff, image/jpeg, text/html, etc.

* **Source**

A reference to a resource from which the present resource is derived in whole or in part. For archival collections, this should be the name of the collection from which the item originates.

The following additional Dublin Core elements are optional, but their use is encouraged:

* **Contributor**

An entity responsible for making contributions to the content of the resource.

* **Relation**

A reference to a related resource.

* **Language**

A language of the intellectual content of the resource. Values should be taken from the *ISO 639-2 standard,* and expressed as three letter codes (i.e., eng, fre).

* **Type**

The nature or genre of the content of the resource. Use standardized vocabularies such as the *Library of Congress Thesaurus for Graphic Materials II: Genre and Physical Characteristic Terms (TGM II)* or the *Art and Architecture Thesaurus.*

* **Rights**

Information about rights held in and over the resource, such as a statement of copyright or other property rights.

Chapter 13
Advanced Bar Code Technology

13.1 Introduction to Bar Code Technology

We live in an information age characterized by rapid change. Today's world moves faster than earlier eras, and the pace continues to speed up. Continuous developments with computer technology in manufacturing, distribution, communications, transportation, healthcare and other sectors have played, and continue to play, a large part in accelerating change.

13.2 Barcode

From an original idea patented in the USA in 1952 by [Woodland and Silver], barcode really became commercialised in the late 1960s in the USA, driven by two key industries, the Grocery/Food/Supermarket sector and the US railways. Work in the grocery sector eventually resulted in the UPC code which was first used in 1974. (A packet of Wrigleys chewing gum was the very first item to be read).Since the first use in 1974, the UPC code became extended to include 2 extra digits to become EAN, which is now probably the most widely used code in the world. Barcode really started to be taken up by industry in 1981 when the US Department of Defence adopted Code 39 for the coding of military equipment.

As time went on, further coding systems were developed and today there are a wide range of different symbologies, available to users.

Barcode is the most widely used identification technology in the world and nowadays there can't be many people on the planet who don't know what a barcode is. It is a very powerful technology, very cheap to produce with a wide range of scanning and printing equipment available in the market at competitive prices. Blackroc provides a wide range of barcode scanning equipment which you can find in the products section of this website.

There are those who consider that barcode has had it's day and that RFID tags will soon replace it. This is a very limited view. It is unlikely that barcode will be replaced by RFID certainly for identification at item level, and in the future it is likely that the two technologies will be used side by side, utilising the different strengths of each to suit particular requirements within the same application.

How does it work?

A traditional (linear) barcode label consists of a series of black and white bars of different widths arranged according to a specific set of rules for that particular barcode type or "symbology". A light source from a barcode reader or "scanner" (CCD or laser), illuminates the label, and receiving optics in the scanner head record the returned light signal from the white spaces which reflect the light and the black bars which absorb the light. These reflected peaks and troughs are converted into electronic signals which are then decoded according to the rules for that particular symbology, into ASCII characters.

Many different linear symbologies are available nowadays, including the following:

UPC-Based Symbologies

* *UPC-A*: Used with consumer products in U.S., 12 characters
* *UPC-E*: Short version of UPC symbol, 6 characters
* *EAN-13*: Used with consumer products internationally, 13 characters
* *EAN-8*: Short version of EAN-13, 8 characters
* *JAN Codes*: Same as EAN-13, used in Japan

* Bookland: Used to mark books with ISBN number
* UPC-Based Extensions
* *2-Digit Ext.*: Used to indicate magazines and newspaper issue numbers
* *5-Digit Ext.*: Used to mark suggested retail price of books
* *2 of 5 Symbologies*:
* *Standard 2 of 5*: Used in airline ticket marking, photofinishing
* *Industrial 2 of 5*: Same as Standard 2 of 5
* *Interleaved 2 of 5*: Used in warehouse, industrial applications
* *Pulse Width Modulated Symbologies*:
* *Plessey Code*: Old symbology, used for shelf marking in retail enviornments
* *MSI*: Variation of Plessey code, with similar applications
* *Modified Plessey Code*: Same as MSI
* *Anker Code*: Used in European POS systems before EAN was implementated
* *Code 11 (USD-8)*: Used to identify telecommunications equipment
* *Postnet*: Printed by U.S. Post Office on envelopes
* *Codabar (aka Ames Code/USD-4/NW-7/2 of 7 Code)*: Used in libraries and blood banks

Check Character : A character used to check the integrity of the preceding bar code symbol. A check character is normally found at the end of the data encoded within the bar code.

Clear Area : The area which precedes the first printed bar of the start character, and follows the last printed bar of the stop character. This area should be free from any printing, and should be of the same color and reflectance as the background of bar code symbol. The clear area should be ten times the width of the narrowest element in the bar code, or 0.25 inch minimum. *Clear Area* is also known as *Quiet Zone*.

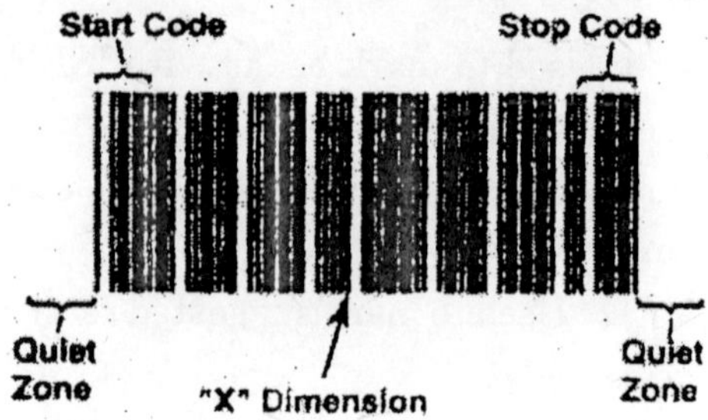

Code 39 : An alphanumeric bar code that can encode decimal numbers, the upper case alphabet, and the following special symbols: _ . * $ / % + Also see *Extended Code 39.*

Codabar : A01234B.

Codabar is a discrete, numeric code with special characters and four different start/stop characters. Allowable data characters are (0 - 9), special characters (- $: / . +), and start-stop characters (A, B, C, D).

Code 128 is a continuous, multilevel, full ASCII code. There are three types of code 128 encoding. Type A provides the character set of all upper case alphanumeric characters plus all of the ASCII control characters. Type B provides the character set of all upper and lower case alphanumeric characters. Type C provides increased density for numeric encoding with double density numeric characters for all number pairs from 00 to 99.

Code 11 : A numeric, high density code.

Code 93 : A continuous, multilevel, full ASCII bar code.

13.3 Advanced Barcode Technology

Advanced Barcode Technology® (ABT) offers innovative, cost-effective automatic identification solutions that enhance business productivity, management control, and the availability of mission-critical information in today's complex, highly competitive business environment.

ABT delivers complete, end to end solutions incorporating their ABT experience in the manufacturing of

Barcode scanning equipment. Combined with leading edge software design backed by superior service and consultation expertise.

THE ABT APPLICATION SUITE FOR MANAGING BUSINESS RESOURCES

ABT provides a complete suite of Windows-based applications , including inventory, business assets, equipment on loan, the job production cycle, and human resources. Each application can be implemented with hand-held devices as a portable automatic identification solution with complete data synchronization. And to help meet the information needs and scalability requirements of the thriving enterprise, all applications in the ABT application suite can be easily integrated with other Windows-based programs, including Microsoft Access and Excel, Oracle, SAP, MySQL, and even AS/400.

13.4 Barcodes – Smart and Dumb

Simply, SMART barcodes have the title and local call number printed on the individual barcode, DUMB barcodes do not.

More specifically, SMART barcodes are usually used in the first stages of automation. They are the product of sending out your shelf list for a Retrospective Conversion or getting your data back in MARC format from any kind of conversion. Usually, barcodes, data disks (which have the matching barcode numbers as part of the new MARC records) and the shelf list are returned at the same time. The idea is to get the barcodes on your books before you start using a computer and barcode scanner at the checkout desk.

On the other hand, DUMB barcodes are usually supplied for ongoing, in-house library use, after the Retrospective Conversion, as things need to be cataloged in the automation system. A 10,000 volume collection may get 10,000 smart barcodes for immediate use and another 3,000 DUMB barcodes for ongoing use for future items that will be added to the collection.

Perhaps the most important thing about SMART barcodes is that before SMART barcodes are printed into sheets or rolls of barcodes with the titles on them, they are sorted (by computer) in your library's local call number order. That means, ideally, the barcodes on the peel-off sheets or rolls are in *better* order than the books on the shelves; or, to put it another way, it means that relatively untrained people can go down your shelves, putting the right barcodes on the right books. In Texas, they have Barcode Parties with the PTO. Elsewhere, there are Trustee volunteers, Honor Student Projects, faculty afterschool task forces (with plenty of refreshments), and Adopt-a-Shelf schemes. Not to mention the solo librarian just doing it, her- or himself.

13.5 Handheld Scanners

These devices are available in two principal technology formats, laser scanners and CCD scanners.

Laser scanners work by moving a tiny beam of laser light (using an oscillating mirror) in a straight line across a barcode and reading the returned light signals. Considered generally as the premier scanning technology, laser light can be emitted to a considerable distance, and so it is the technology of choice for long range applications, and scanners are available which can read up to 10 metres or so. Because the beam of laser light is linear, for use with 2D barcodes a laser scanning beam has to be "rastered", that is, moved up and down the label in order to get 2D coverage.

CCD scanners work by illuminating the barcode label with a thin line of light usually from an array of LEDs in the head of the scanner, and then taking an image of the illuminated line, on a pixel by pixel basis and then decoding the light and dark spaces. CCDs are either linear, that is they read a thin line of light, for use with linear barcodes, or area, that is they can take an image of the whole area (e.g. for 2D barcodes), a bit like using a CCD camera. Because the latter works like a CCD camera it can also be used for capturing non-barcode images such as signatures and peoples faces for example, (often also referred to as imagers). In general terms CCD scanners tend to be cheaper than laser scanners.

^ back to top of page

13.6 What do I Need to Print Barcodes?

Dot matrix, laser, and ink jet printers can be used to print barcode labels, but they all have their drawbacks. Thermal label printers are specifically designed for the task and so give the best results. They can print at high speeds and can be used to print single labels at a time, or whole rolls at once.

Thermal Printing Explained

Thermal printing involves heat transfer from a thermal printhead to a heat sensitive paper or ribbon. The printhead consists of a long, linear array of tiny resistive heating elements that are arranged perpendicular to the flow of the paper. Each element heats the area directly below it on the paper and the image is produced by the rows of dots that are printed onto the paper as it passes beneath the printhead.

There are two basic thermal printing methods:

Direct Thermal Printing (DT) : With this method, the printhead is in direct contact with the chemically treated paper and no ribbon is used. As a result, the running costs are lower, however, this method will also wear down the printhead faster than with thermal transfer as paper is coarse and will wear the printhead down over time. In addition to this the edge of each label strikes the printhead as it passes causing further wear. So although no ribbon is needed, the printhead will wear out faster. Printheads are considered to be consumables and must be included in the overall cost of operation.

This method should be used where the lifecycle of the label is very short, and cannot come into contact with heat or ultra violet light. Thermal paper will mark if scratched and will eventually turn black if left for long periods of time.

Chapter 14
RFID Technology

14.1 What is RFID (Radio Frequency Identification)?

In the 21st Century, libraries will operate with such simplicity that users will be able to check materials in and out themselves and find what they want almost instantly - leaving library staff with more time to give users the personal attention so many of them need and to keep up with the avalanche of new information and materials being created every day.

RFID, or Radio Frequency Identification, is one of the most exciting new library technologies in years. It promises to revolutionize how librarians do their work and how customers receive library services.

In general terms, Radio Frequency Identification (RFID) is a means of identifying a person or an object by using a radio frequency transmission. These wireless automatic identification data capture systems allow for non-contact reading or writing of data, and they are highly effective in manufacturing and other hostile environments where bar code labels cannot survive.

RFID has been in existence for over 20-years, and it has been extensively used in applications such as tool collection, access control and/or ticketing. In recent years, the technology has received increased attention due to a confluence of events including technology advancement, heightened security concerns, supply chain automation, and a continuing emphasis on cost control within industrial systems.

RFID (Radio Frequency IDentification) is the latest technology to be used in library theft detection systems. Unlike EM (Electro-Mechanical) and RF (Radio Frequency) systems, which have been used in libraries for decades, RFID-based systems move beyond security to become tracking systems that combine security with more efficient tracking of materials throughout the library, including easier and faster charge and discharge, inventorying, and materials handling.

RFID is the complete security and inventory management package for modern libraries. Librarians need systems and technologies that help reduce their workload. One such technology is Radio Frequency Identification (RFID) tags for books and materials. The technology works through flexible, paper-thin smart labels that are incorporated into ultra small RFID chips. These smart labels can be applied directly on library books and can be read with a RFID scanner. Line of sight is not essential for reading the tags with the scanner. Therefore, the tags may be placed in different locations on the books.

RFID is a combination of radio -frequency-based technology and microchip technology. The information contained on microchips in the tags affixed to library materials is read using radio frequency technology regardless of item orientation or alignment (i.e., the technology does not require line-of-sight or a fixed plane to read tags as do traditional theft detection systems) and distance from the item is not a critical factor except in the case of extra-wide exit gates. The corridors at the building exit(s) can be as wide as four feet because the tags can be read at a distance of up to two feet by each of two parallel exit sensors. [The devices used for circulation and inventorying are usually called "readers" while the ones used at building exits are usually called "sensors."]

Radio frequency identification (RFID) is one of the most rapidly growing segments of today's information technology (IT) and automatic identification and data capture industries. Many large library around the world have implemented RFID to speed material check-in, checkout, shelf inventory, and security application. Low-cost, flexible smart labels are inserted in books and can be made invisible to patrons. Counter personal can check dozens of books in or out in mere seconds without manually handling and orienting each item. The tags also can be used for theft detection, much like anti-shoplifting technology currently used by retailers. Librarians using portable computers with RFID readers can take inventory and find misfiled materials simply by walking down an aisle of bookshelves. The reader can automatically detect missing materials and alert the operator.

RFID uses low-power radio signals to exchange data wirelessly between chips and reader/encoders. No direct line of sight is needed between the tag and read/write device, eliminating many of the labor and item-orientation requirements associated with other forms of automated data collection. RFID readers can simultaneously recognize and process hundreds of tags within their read fields, while barcodes have to be scanned one by one.

14.2 How is RFID Different than Bar Code?

It is important to understand the significant differences between RFID and bar code to appreciate the benefits RFID can provide. Bar code and RFID are both identification technologies that hold data that is accessed by some type of reader. In actuality, they complement each other very well and can be used effectively side by side in many applications. Bar code is an optical technology and RDID is a radio technology. The ways these technologies exchange data account for most of the differences between RFID and bar code and help determine where each identification technology is best put to use.

As a radio technology, RFID requires no line-of-sight between the reader and the tag to exchange data. RFID tags therefore can be read through packaging, including cardboard containers and plastic wrap used to seal pallets. FRID is subject to interference however, particularly from metal, so potential sources of interference must be recognized and accounted for during system planning.

RFID readers can automatically recognize and

differentiate all the RF tags in their reading fields. This simultaneous processing capability provides additional flexibility for material handling, packaging and sortation operations because there is no need to maintain spacing between objects to ensure they will be read. The ability to read dozens or even hundreds of tags per second makes RFID ideal for high-speed sortation, receiving, cross docking and other applications.

14.3 Component of RFID System

A comprehensive RFID system has three components:

(1) RFID tags

(2) Reader or sensors

(3) Antenna

(4) Server/Docking Station

14.3.1 RFID Tags

It composed of a microchip attached to an antenna that is packaged in a way that it can be applied to an object. The tag picks up signals from and sends signals to a reader. Tags can be smaller than a grain of rice or as large as a brick. RFID tags are either passive (no battery) or active (self-powered by a battery) or semi-passive. Data transmission speed and range depend on the radio frequency, antenna size, power output, and interference. Tag can be read-only, read-write and WORM.

In "passive" tags are the most common tags used for libraries. In this system the power to read the tags comes from the reader or sensor, rather than from a battery within the tag. In "active" tags, which have their own power supply, are substantially larger and more expensive than the tags used in library RFID applications. It is these tags that can be read at distances of up to ten feet.

For library, tags have been specifically designed to be applied on to library media including books, CDs, DVDs and taps.

Features

* The RFID tag has 3 sections: a lockable section for the item identification, a re-writable one for library specific use, and a security function for the item antitheft.
* The RFID tag don't need to be visible to be read: books and other media can be quickly identified in any orientation.
* The RFID chip integrates a "multi-read" function, allowing several items to be processed simultaneously.
* The RFID tags are compatible with traditional library security systems.
* The RFID tags are self-adhesive and can be affixed directly onto items. They come in different forms: rectangular for books, round for CDs, long for audiocassettes. They can be easily attached to paper labels.

TECHNICAL SPECIFICATIONS

Here are the common types of passive RFID tags and their performance characteristics:

* Low Frequency RFID systems operate at about 125 kHz with a typical maximum read of up to 20 inches (508 mm).
* High Frequency FRID systems operate at 13.56 MHz with a typical maximum read range of up to 3 feet (1 meter).
* Ultra-High Frequency RFID systems operate at multiple frequencies, including 868 MHz (in Europe), a band centered at 915 MHz, and 2.45 GHz (microwave). Read range is typically 3 to 10 feet (1 to 3 meters), but systems operating in the 915 MHz band may achieve read ranges of 20 feet (6 meters) or more.
* Delivery packaging in rolls of 2000 self-adhesive labels

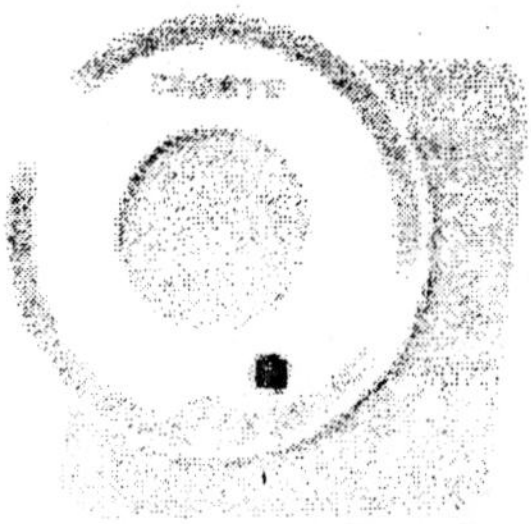

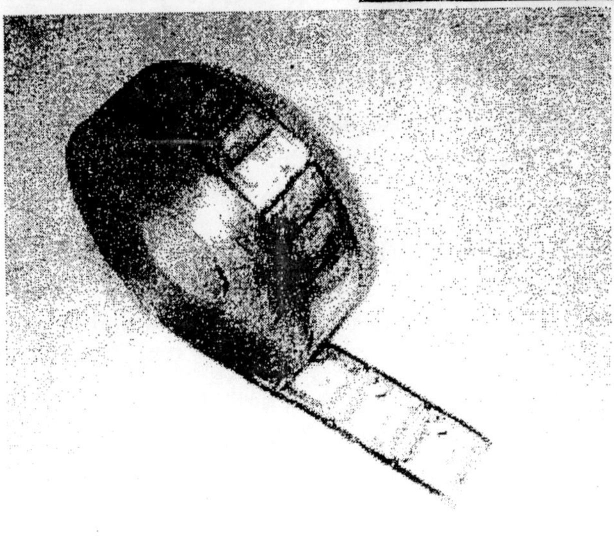

> Have longer life spans than barcodes.
> Multi-read abilities allow batch processing.
> Utilizes low cost 13.56 MHz frequency.
> Incorporates an anti-theft capability.

14.3.2 RFID Reader

A typical system includes several different kinds of readers, also known as sensors when installed at library exits. These are radio frequency devices designed to detect and read tags to obtain the information stored thereon. The reader powers an antenna to generate an RF field. When a tag passes through the field, the information stored on the chip in the tag is decoded by the reader and sent to the server which, in turn, communicates with the automated library system when the RFID system is interfaced with it. While there is software in each reader to facilitate communication with the server and/or with library staff, most of the software supplied by the RFID system vendor is on the server when one is included in the system. When there is no server, most of the software is on the readers, although some may be on a docking station.

It connected to a computer, which takes the place of a bar code scanner. It can also be battery powered to allow mobile transactions with RFID tags.

The reader is also sometimes called an interrogator because it "interrogates" the tag.

Features

* The handheld RFID/Barcode reader can perform three operations: scan the barcode, program the RFID tag and activate/de-activate the antitheft function of the RFID tag.
* It is a convenient tool to help libraries move from a barcode system to an RFID system. It provides the necessary flexibility for a smooth transition to RFID and is the ideal product for the management of inter-library loans.

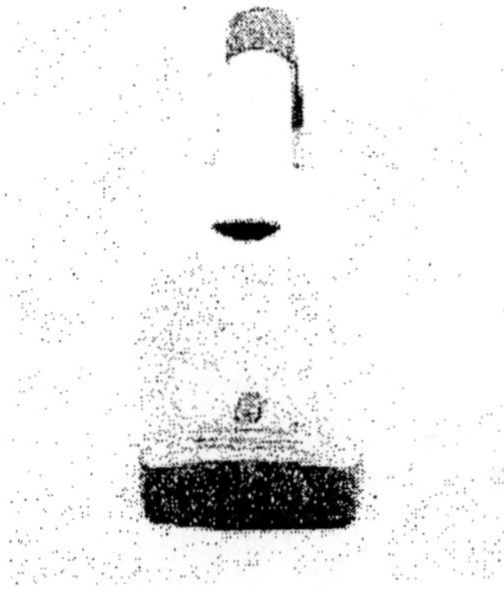

14. 3 RFID Antenna

RFID Antenna connected to the reader, which has a size and a structure that is determined by the distance for communicating and performing at a given stage.

The tag antenna is the conductive element that enables the tag to send and receive data. Passive, low- (135 kHz) and high-frequency (13.56 MHz) tags usually have a coiled antenna that couples with the coiled antenna of the reader to form a magnetic field. UHF tag antennas can be a variety of shapes. Readers also have antennas which are used to emit radio waves. The RF energy from the reader antenna is "harvested" by the antenna and used to power up the microchip, which then changes the electrical load on the antenna to reflect back its own signals.

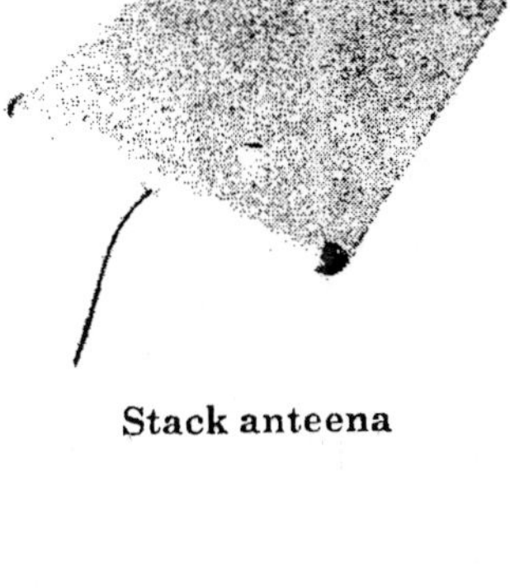

Stack anteena

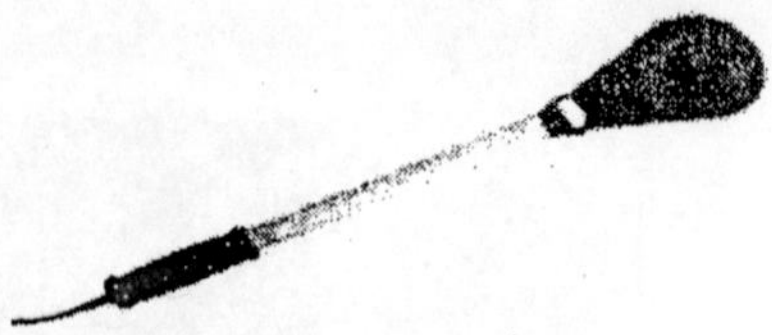

Library wand 1 Anteena

14.3.4 Server/Docking Station

It is the communications gateway among the various components. It receives the information from one or more of the readers and exchanges information with the circulation database. The server typically includes a transaction database so that reports can be produced.

The server is the heart of some comprehensive RFID systems. It is the communications gateway among the various components. It receives the information from one or more of the readers and exchanges information with the circulation database. Its software includes the APIs (Applications Programming Interface) necessary to interface it with the automated library system. The server typically includes a transaction database so that reports can be produced. A server costs as much as $15,000, more than two-thirds of which is the software.

14.4 Staff Check-Out Station

The self checkout station allows patrons to borrow books without assistance from the library staff.

- Self Service
- Convenience
- Privacy
- Eliminates bottlenecks
- Very easy to learn
- No orientation issues
- Productivity factors

* Frees staff
* Online updating of central database
* Theft system disarmed
* Option of writing other information to tag
* Transaction(s) could be linked to security camera
* Receipt issued

14.5 Self-Return Book Drop with Automatic check-in Feature Station

The self-return book drop, in turn, allows loans to be cancelled instantly as patrons deposit books through an external book return chute. This interface also updates the database and alerts the library when items are returned.

* Very Fast
* Multiple items
* Multiple Media
* Any orientation
* Situated within library or at a remote location
* External access
* Internal access
* Books returned are immediately updated on the central database

14.6 Shelving Station

The shelving station tells the staff where to reshelf the book and also activates the security bit. The Fastrac Modular Sorting System is a revolutionary system that takes the materials from the return chute, checks them in, sorts them and distributes them to multiple bins, areas, or even floors for re-shelving. With continuous book handling, using a system that supports hundreds of bins, Fastrac can process over 2000 items per hour. It can sort items by status or bookshelf location and redirect accordingly. Rapid processing and automated efficiencies means "shorter to shelf" periods and less work for library staff.

14.7 Library Security Gates

The library security system benefits from the latest design innovations to combine both item identification and security into a single device: the RFID Tag. The VTLS Security Gates feature the most modern detection algorithm that constantly detects non de-activated antitheft function.

During check-out and check-in operations, the antitheft function is automatically de-activated or activated at the same time. Items that have not been checked out properly instantaneously trigger the gate's alarm as they pass through the detection field.

14.7.1 Features

* Each pedestal is standalone and plug and play to the main power, and does not require additional equipment.
* Featuring an advance Digital Signal Processing technology, prove maximum detection speed and field, regardless of the RFID tag orientation.
* Security Gate is made of 2 pedestals. Additional pedestals can be added in a row for increased detection surface.
* Security Gate need not to be linked to the library database, and therefore they can still operate when the Library network is down or overloaded.
* Security system uses a single RFID tag for both identification and security, as well as a single piece of

hardware equipment, to offer an efficient, reliable and cost-effective solution.

14.7.2 Technical specifications

Components:2 parts, 1 pedestal, includes an antenna set for large detection field, 1 electronic unit (controller) for each pedestal.

Size (L x W x H): Pedestal = 560 x 530 x 1630 mm (22 x 2 x 64 inches), Controller = 180 x 380 x 80 mm (7x15x3inches)

Weight: Pedestal = 23 kg (50.7 lbs)

Controller = 2.2 kg. (4.8 lbs)

Materials: Plastic enclosure: ABS – UL 94 VO, can be replaced with non-conductive materials

Color: Light gray, Pantone 536C

14.8 Inventory Control System

Lets you take inventory and locate missing items. The RFID Inventory Control System consists of two parts: 1) a hand-held RFID reader that you can use to scan items on your shelves and 2) software developed by VTLS that lets you generate inventory reports about the collected data. The RFID Inventory Control System speeds up the inventory process, locates misshelved items, and improves inventory accuracy.

* No line of sight
* Books on shelves or stacked
* No handling except for misplaced books
* Speed is the payoff

* Implementers indicate a 75% reduction in human resource required for shelf management activities

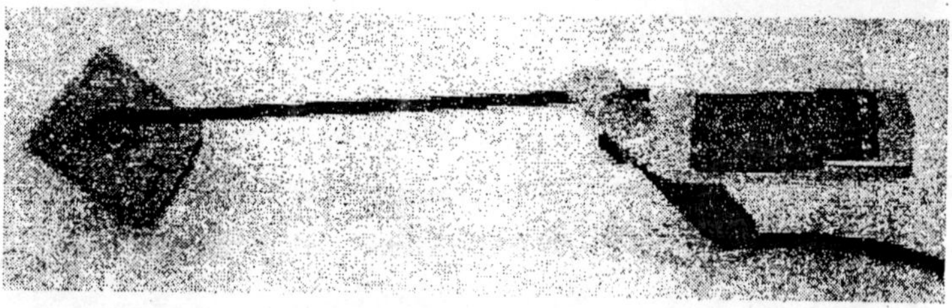

14.9 Benefits of RFID in Automated Library

The RFID Solution provides numerous advantages over traditional barcode systems. Here are just a few of the benefits:

* **Rapid charging/discharging**

The use of RFID reduces the amount of time required to perform circulation operations. The most significant time savings are attributable to the facts that information can be read from RFID tags much faster than from barcodes and that several items in a stack can be read at the same time.

* RFID is a comprehensive system that combines RFID security and the tracking of materials throughout the library; or it is a hybrid system that uses EM for security and RFID for tracking, but handles both simultaneously with a single piece of equipment. The time savings are less for charging than for discharging because the time required for charging usually is extended by social interaction with patrons

* **Simplified patron self-charging/discharging**

For patrons using self-charging, there is a marked improvement because they do not have to carefully place materials within a designated template and they can charge several items at the same time.

* Patron self-discharging shifts that work from staff to patrons. Staff is relieved further when readers are installed in bookdrops.

* **High reliability**

The readers are highly reliable. Anecdotal evidence suggests that is the case whenever a reader is within 12 to 14 inches of the tags, but there appears to be no statistical data to support the claims.

* Some RFID systems have an interface between the exit sensors and the circulation system to identify the items moving out of the library. Were a patron to run out of the library and not be intercepted, the library would at least know what had been stolen. If the patron card also has an RFID tag, the library will also be able to determine who removed the items without properly charging them.

* **High-speed inventorying**

A unique advantage of RFID systems is their ability to scan books on the shelves without tipping them out or removing them. A hand-held inventory reader can be moved rapidly across a shelf of books to read all of the unique identification information. Using wireless technology, it is possible not only to update the inventory, but also to identify items which are out of proper order.

* **Long tag life**

Finally, RFID tags last longer than barcodes because nothing comes into contact with them. Most RFID vendors claim a minimum of 100,000 transactions before a tag may need to be replaced.

14.10 Disadvantages of RFID Systems

* **High cost**

The major disadvantage of RFID technology is its cost. While the readers and sensors used to read the information are comparable in cost to the components of a typical EM or RF theft detection system, typically $2,500 to $3,500 or more each; a server costing as much as $15,000 may be required and the tags cost $.60 to $.85 each. It may be some time before the cost of tags comes down to $.50 or lessskepticism in the industry.

* **Vulnerability to compromise**

It is possible to compromise an RFID system by wrapping the protected material in two to three layers of ordinary household foil to block the radio signal.

* It is also possible to compromise an RFID system by placing two items against one another so that one tag overlays another. That may cancel out the signals. This requires knowledge of the technology and careful alignment.

* **Removal of exposed tags**

3M, which recommends EM for security and RFID for tracking, argues that EM strips are concealed in the spines (30 percent of customers) or the gutters (70 percent of customers) of books and are, therefore, difficult to find and remove; while RFID tags are typically affixed to the inside back cover and are exposed for removal. If a library wishes, it can insert the RFID tags in the spines of all except thin books, however, not all RFID tags are flexible enough. A library can also imprint the RFID tags with its logo and make them appear to be bookplates, or it can put a printed cover label over each tag.

Exit sensor problems

While the short-range readers used for circulation charge and discharge and inventorying appear to read the tags 100 percent of the time, the performance of the exit sensors is more problematic. They must read tags at up to twice the distance of the other readers.

Perceived Invasion of Patron Privacy

There is a perception among some that RFID is a threat to patron privacy. That perception is based on two misconceptions: (1) that the tags contain patron information and (2) that they can be read after someone has taken the materials to home or office.

* The vast majority of the tags installed in library materials contain only the item ID, usually the same number that previously has been stored on a barcode.

14.11 How it Reduces Staff Workload

* Processes more items in a shorter period of time with less handling
* Accurate multi-item self-check circulation in patron's preferred language
* Rapid real-time or batch inventories that leverage ILS reporting
* Wireless weeding
* Book returns that do the work for you with automatic check-in
* Automatic sorting that distributes material to multiple bins, areas, or even floors for reshelving and "shorter to shelf' periods
* Offline transactions are automatically updated with no staff intervention

Appendices

A. Glossary of Terms

Glossary of Terms

– A –

Access Point

A name, term, code, etc., under which a book or other item may be searched and identified in the catalog, for example: author, title, subject, call number.

API - Application Programming Interface

An interface between the operating system and application programs, which includes the way applications communicate with the operating system, and the services the operating system makes available to programs.

Architecture

Design, or the way components fit together. It can be used to describe any system, as in "software architecture" or "network architecture".

Authentication

Verification of identity for security purposes. Passwords and digital signatures are forms of authentication.

Authority Control

A method to control the number of similar headings (usually subjects or authors) in the library catalog. Multiple entries are cross-referenced to a single entry using authority control.

Automation

Automatic, as opposed to human, operation or control of a process, equipment or a system; or the techniques and equipment used to achieve this. In libraries, automation refers to the process of automating functions such as circulation, cataloging, or acquisitions.

– B –

Barcode

A printed horizontal strip of vertical bars used for identifying specific items or users. The codes, which represent numerical data, are read by a bar code reader and interpreted via software or hardware decoders. In libraries, barcodes are affixed to both books and library cards to assist in circulation and collection control.

Boolean Operators

Words such as AND, OR, and NOT used to broaden or narrow a search. For example, **cats AND dogs** narrows the search to titles about both cats and dogs, while **cats OR dogs** broadens the search.

Browse Searching

A feature of a catalog which allows the user to search by the first word in a field, not a word appearing anywhere in the field. Compare to Keyword Searching.

– C –

CGI Script

A computer program, most frequently written in C, Perl, or a shell script, that uses the Common Gateway Interface (CGI) standard to provide an interactive interface between a user or an application and a Web server. CGI script is most commonly used to develop forms that allow users to submit information to a Website.

Character Set

A standard collection of characters. A character set may include letters, digits, punctuation, control codes, graphics, mathematical symbols, and other signs. Each character in the set is represented by a unique character code, which is a binary number used for storage and transmission.

Chat Room

An online space where two or more people can input (usually via keyboard) messages to a group of people who are logged in at the same time. Compare to Message Forum

Client

A computer system or process that requests a service of another computer system or process (see Server). For example, a workstation requesting a file from a server is a client of the file server.

Client/Server

A common type of distributed system in which software is split between server tasks and client tasks. A client sends requests to a server asking for information or action, and the server responds. There may be either one centralized server or many distributed ones.

Codabar

A specific type of bar code used in libraries, blood banks, the overnight package delivery industry, and a variety of other information processing applications. It is also known as USD-4, NW-7, and 2 of 7 code. See Barcode.

Command Line Interface

A means of communication between a program and its user in which commands are input with a keyboard and are interpreted and executed by the program. Results are output as text or graphics on the computer screen. Compare to Graphical User Interface.

Cookie

Data created on your own computer when you access certain Web pages. Usually the cookie keeps information about your preferences and reuses this information when you access that site again, thus "recognizing" repeat visitors. Cookies cannot be used to access any other data on your computer, nor can they determine your e-mail address or identity. You can set your browser to reject all cookies or to warn you before accepting cookies, but sites that provide personalized services, such as stock trading sites or shopping carts, won't work if you don't accept cookies.

– D –

Database

A structured set of data, generally accessed via a software program. A simple database might be a single file containing many records, each of which contains the same set of fields, such as a series of companies with name, address, phone, and contact fields for each one.

Database Management System (DBMS)

Complex set of programs that control the organization, storage and retrieval of data for many users. Data is organized in fields, records and files. Examples include Oracle, Sybase, and Datacom.

Dedicated Line

A permanent connection between computers using telephone, ISDN, or other types of lines.

Dialup

A temporary, as opposed to dedicated, connection between machines established over a telephone line using modems. A patron might use a dialup connection from home (using a personal computer, modem, and telephone line) to dial into and use the library catalog.

Digital Document

Books, articles, papers, etc., that can be accessed via a computer.

Digital Media

Media in various digital forms, including scanned images, audio, video, multimedia, drawings and intelligent documents.

Domain Name System (DNS)

The unique name of a collection of computers connected to a network such as the Internet. A replicated, distributed data query service for looking up host IP addresses based on host names. The DNS is hierarchical, consisting of domains, subdomains, sites, and hosts. Unique names are formed from smallest to largest, and are of the form *user@host.site.subdomain.domain*, where *host* and *site* are often optional. On the Internet, domain names typically end with a suffix denoting the type of site:

* **.com** (commercial)
* **.edu** (educational)
* **.net** (network operations)
* **.gov**(US government)
* **.mil** (US military)
* **.org** (organization)
* **.us** (United States)
* **.ca** (Canada)
* **.uk** (United Kingdom)
* **.au** (Australia)
* **.cz** (Czech Republic)
* **.xx**(where ***xx*** refers to another country's two-letter abbreviation)

Download

To copy a file from an external computer to a local one. You may download software updates from a vendor to your library system via the Internet.

Dublin Core

A minimal set of metadata elements used to describe networked information resources which aids users in locating specific items.

Dumb Terminal

An output device (not a computer) that contains no internal microprocessor; a display monitor with no processing capabilities.

– E –

EAD

Encoded Archival Description is the emerging standard for archival finding aids and is used by Library of Congress and other research institutions. Finding aids are inventories, registers, indexes, or guides that provide detailed information about specific collections. Standardizing the format of these tools makes it easier to display them on a network.

EDIFACT (ISO 9735)

Electronic data interchange (EDI) refers to any electronic commerce standard that defines a protocol for exchange of business data between software applications. EDIFACT (EDI for Administration, Commerce, and Transport) is the international standard for EDI.

Encryption

The process of scrambling a message so that a key, held only by authorized recipients, is needed to unscramble and read the message.

Ethernet

Computers on the Internet that use the TCP/IP protocols are frequently connected to the Net over an Ethernet link. Ethernet supports communications at 10 mbps over several types of wiring. An Ethernet card connects an individual computer to a network.

Extranet

An extended intranet connecting not only internal personnel, but also select customers, suppliers, and strategic partners. Compare to Internet and Intranet.

– F –

FAQ — Frequently Asked Questions

Web page or text file with common questions about various topics along with the answers. Especially useful for first-time visitors to a site or new participants in a newsgroup or listserv.

Filtering software

A program to block access to certain Web pages. Depending on the program, it may block certain specified sites, all sites with certain words, or it may use more sophisticated criteria to determine which pages to block. See the LibraryHQ's Internet Filtering and Blocking page.

Firewall

A gateway used to protect a server or a network from unauthorized access. A firewall generally consists of both hardware and software components.

– G –

Graphical User Interface (GUI)

The use of pictures rather than just words to represent

the input and output of a program. The program displays icons, buttons, dialog boxes etc. in its windows on the screen; the user controls it by moving a mouse or pointer on the screen, selecting objects by pressing buttons on the mouse. Compare to Command Line Interface.

– H –

HTML

Hypertext Markup Language is the set of codes (or tags) inserted in a file intended for display on a Web browser. The codes tell the Web browser how to display the words and images on the page.

Hypertext

Text on a Web page that, when clicked on, jumps the reader to another page or image.

– I –

Inter Library Loan(ILL)

A library activity which lends on loan documents required by other library users.

Integrated Library System (ILS)

An automated library system in which all of the functional modules (acquisitions, circulation, cataloging, serials, an OPAC, etc.) are accessible online and share a common machine-readable database. An automated library system is considered integrated only if all library functions are processed against a single, master bibliographic file.

Imported/Exported Bibliography Records

Because of the standards established for the creation and transferal of library bibliographic records, libraries can exchange records through import and export.

Interface

In hardware, an interface is a connector used to link devices. In software, it allows communication between two software systems or between people and systems. In the automation field, interface refers to the method by which users can access the automated library system. See Graphical User Interface.

Internet

A network of networks; a group of networks interconnected via routers. The Internet is the world's largest network.

Internet Service Provider

A company that provides other companies or individuals with access to, or a presence on, the Internet.

Intranet

A network of computers and servers accessed via Web browsers, but maintained within an organization or company, and not generally accessible to those outside the organization.

ISBN (ISO 2108)

International Standard Book Number: a unique numerical 10-digit identifier for a published title. It helps to ensure more efficient ordering, inventory control, and accounting.

ISSN (ISO 3297)

International Standard Serial Number: identifies serial publications including monographic series. In 1979 the ISSN replaced the ISBN for serials.

– J –

Java

A programming language designed so that its object modules can run on many different platforms. Java is often used to create *applets*, or Web-based programs that run when a user accesses the page or clicks on a certain area.

JavaScript

A scripting language used to create *scripts*, or small programs embedded in Web pages that run when a user accesses the page or clicks on a certain area.

– K –

Keyword Searching

A keyword search looks for specific words or terms that occur anywhere in a field (title, subject, heading, contents, etc.). Keyword searching is useful when you have incomplete information. Compare to Browse Searching.

– L –

LAN – Local Area Network

A geographically limited data communications network that connects several computers. Library automation systems require a LAN to enable all users to access the same database.

Legacy System

An older computer system or program that is still valuable to the user, but may not be compatible with newer systems.

Licensing

An automation system requires the library to obtain a user license, as with any type of software. Licenses are usually purchased as either a site license, which allows the library to install the automation software on as many computers desired within a single building, or on a per-computer or per-network basis.

Listserv

A Listserv is a program that automatically redistributes e-mail to names on a mailing list. Users can subscribe, unsubscribe, and send messages to everyone on the list by sending notes to a specific email address.

– M –

MARC - (Machine-Readable Cataloging)

MARC refers to (1) a computer record structure, (2) a set of tags and indicators to identify parts of the record, (3) the level of cataloging information contained in the Library of Congress's MARC records, and (4) the body of records distributed by the Library of Congress MARC Distribution Service.

Message Forum

Also called a Message Board. An online space where people can leave messages that become visible to anyone who accesses the forum. Compare to Chat Room.

Module/Application Module

A module is a software segment that performs a specific function, such as acquisitions or circulation. Automation system vendors may sell modules separately, though circulation and cataloging modules are often sold together, with add-on modules as possible extra purchases.

– N –

NetPC, NetworkPC

A computer with minimal memory, disk storage and processor power designed to connect to and work via a network.

Network

A group of interconnected computers, including the

hardware, software, and cabling used to connect them.

Newsgroups

see Usenet Newsgroups

NISO

A nonprofit association accredited as a standards developer by the American National Standards Institute, the national clearinghouse for voluntary standards development in the U.S. NISO has developed standards for Information Retrieval (Z39.50), 12083 (an SGML Tool), Z39.2 (Information Interchange Format), Codes for Languages and Countries, and Z39.18 (Scientific and Technical Reports).

– O –

OCLC

Online Library Computer Center is a large US based bibliographic network activity in library networking.

OPAC

Online Public Access Catalog: provides access to the library's holdings via a computer monitor, replacing the traditional card catalog. May also be called a PAC (Public Access Catalog).

Operating Systems (OS)

The low-level software on a computer that schedules tasks, allocates storage, handles the interface to peripheral hardware, and presents a default interface to the user when no application program is running. Examples: UNIX, Windows98, Windows NT.

– P –

Protocols

Sets of rules or standards that let computers communicate over the Internet. **HTTP** (Hypertext Transfer Protocol) allows transfer of Web pages via a browser. **FTP** (File Transfer Protocol) allows transfer of files through the Internet from one computer to another.

Push Technology

Internet technology that allows information to be delivered or "pushed" directly to a user who subscribes to it. PointCast, Yahoo, and other services provide news to users who can customize their news reports by selecting topics like sports, world news, and business that are entered into a database.

– Q –

Query

A user's request for information from a database or search engine. A query is a search string entered by a patron when searching for a particular library item or subject in the library's catalog, or OPAC.

– R –

RAM

The part of primary storage that holds a software program and small amounts of data when they are brought from secondary storage.

RDBMS

Relational Database Management System. See Relational Database.

Record Conversion

Record conversion is an aspect of retrospective conversion, in which book records on a tape or disk are converted to MARC format for use in an automation system. Conversion is usually processed by the automation system or by an outside vendor specializing in retrospective conversion.

Relational Database

A database in the form of tables having rows and columns to show the relationships between items. If data is changed in one table, it will be changed in all related tables. See Database.

Remote Access

Service allowing users away from the server or network to access these resources from remote locations.

Retrospective Conversion

Retrospective conversion is the process by which libraries convert a shelflist (such as a card catalog) to a searchable, computerized database. This database can then be used as the backbone of an automation system.

Request For Information (RFI)

A formal request that a library prepares and sends to vendors for information on their automation systems.

Request For Proposal (RFP)

A formal open bid document that a library prepares to obtain a customized response from a vendor. Responses may include pricing, enhancements, implementation plan, and timeline. An RFP is usually the precursor to a legal contract between vendor and library.

– S –

SDI

Selective Dissemination of Information is a service by which information is provided to users on the basis of their specific requirements. The service is rendered on basis of user's interest profiles.

Server

A computer that provides some service for other computers connected to it via a network. The library's database containing all book records is located on a server so that several client machines (OPACs) can access the files. See Client/Server.

Site Preparation

The process of installing wiring, cabling, and other support hardware, in addition to planning the placement of computers, terminals, and networks within the library.

System Upgrade

A new or better version of hardware or software, or the act of developing or installing a new version. An automation system upgrade might be the change between a command-line based system and a GUI-based or Web-based automation system.

– T –

TCP/IP

Transmission Control Protocol/Internet Protocol, the suite of communications protocols used to connect computers on the Internet.

Thin Client

A thin client is a machine that only functions when connected to a central server, as compared to a networked PC, which can store and process information on its hard drive.

The function of a thin client is to centralize data transmission and storage in a LAN environment.

Truncation

In searching, truncation means that the system will allow wildcards to extend a search term. For example, a truncated term with a wildcard, such as app*, will retrieve all entries that begin with app, from apples to application. See Wildcard.

Turnkey

A complete hardware and software computer system customized for a particular application, such as library automation. Turnkey systems are fully operational, requiring no additional components or modifications.

– U –

Unicode

A 16-bit, language-independent character set that enables representation of all of the characters commonly used in information processing.

UniMARC

An international MARC format that accepts records created in any of the more than 20 MARC formats, thus facilitating conversion of records among them.

UNIX

Widely used multi-user general-purpose computer operating system.

User interface

The aspects of a computer system or program that can be perceived by the human user, and the commands and mechanisms used to control its operation and input data. See Graphical User Interface and Command Line Interface.

Usenet Newsgroups

Usenet is a collection of messages on various subjects that are posted to servers on a worldwide network. Each subject collection is called a newsgroup. Most newsgroups are hosted on Internet-connected servers, but they can also be hosted from servers that are not part of the Internet.

URL

Uniform Resource Locator: the address a computer uses to locate documents on the Internet.

– V –

Video Display Unit

A device incorporating a display monitor, a keyboard and a serial port. The most common VDUs, "dumb terminals, " are used primarily to send and receive information from a central computer.

Virtual Library

A virtual (as opposed to physical) collection existing only as digital files accessible via computer, not as books or tangible media in a library building.

– W –

WWW

A portion of the internet that uses the transport functions of the internet, via a client/server architecture, to handle all types of digital information, to handle all types of digital information, including text, hypermedia graphics and sound.

Web Browser

Software program that allows you to access Web pages on the Internet, an Intranet, or an Extranet. The two most popular browsers are Microsoft's Internet Explorer and Netscape Navigator.

Wide Area Network (WAN)

A network, usually constructed with serial lines, extending over distances greater than one mile. A library system may use a WAN to connect branch libraries to the greater automation system.

Wildcard

A special character such as *, $, or ? that can replace any character or characters in a string. Wildcards are used in catalog searches to extend a search term. See Truncation.

WindowsNT

Microsoft's 32-bit operating system designed for high-end workstations, servers and corporate networks.

Wizard

An interactive help utility that guides the user through a potentially complex task.

– X –

X12

An Electronic Data Interchange standard — the American equivalent of UN/EDIFACT and various other national and industry EDI messaging protocols.

– Z –

Z39.20

A NISO (National Information Standards Organization) standard for measuring the extent of price changes on a periodic basis for a variety of library materials including hardcover trade and technical books, paperback books, periodicals, and microforms.

Z39.50

A NISO (National Information Standards Organization) standard for information retrieval that allows any library using a Z39.50-compliant automated library system to access remote library collections. Z39.50 specifies a query/response protocol between a client and a server. See LibraryHQ's Z39.50 page.